BREAKFAST AT NOON

Backwards in the 'Burbs

C. R. Yeager

ISBN 0-9770662-0-7 (hardcover)
ISBN 0-9770662-1-5 (paperback)

LCCN 2005928870

Printed in the United States of America

for the women

Happiness and the absurd are two sons of the same earth.

—Camus

Support IDA

Founded by Dr. Samuel T. Orton in 1949, The International Dyslexia Association offers a legacy of resources and encouragement to people of all ages. Contact them at:

The International Dyslexia Association
8600 LaSalle Road
Chester Building, Suite 382
Baltimore, Maryland 21826–2044 USA
410–296–0232
Fax 410–321–5069
1–800–ABCD123
Email: *info@interdys.org*
www.interdys.org

Acknowledgments

Thanks to:

 —Thom Zahler and Dianne Dodd for taking the concept to another dimension;

 —the staff at BookMasters, Inc., especially Tony Parsons, Kristen Butler, and Ryan Feasel, for shepherding the unruly beast into print. The book, also.

Contents

Contents

Introduction: Crossing Both Ways Before I Look

In the house where I grew up, an old barn in Cleveland Heights, Ohio, I spent a lot of time reading in a corner of my bedroom, where two outside walls met. This spot had both good and bad points. There was something delicious about being so comfortable and secure two stories up, inches from the open air. But it also meant being directly above the kitchen counter, where my mother's AM radio blasted *Northwest Orient Airlines* commercials and other drivel that I hated.

Looking back, I realize I've lived a great deal in or at such interfaces, points that offer a double perspective: in suburbia, as spouse, parent, and dyslexic, and as the son of British and American parents. Being a Boomer, a member of the Sandwich Generation, one of the most pivotal ever, has probably reinforced this. The midpoint of my life seems an appropriate time to toast such duality, with as much humor as possible. As the blues, according to Albert King, is a celebration of life's suffering, humor is a way of paying life's tab while picking its pocket. Especially mid-life's, equity-mindedness being a natural, if dubious, by-product of aging.

Introduction

About dyslexia: in case you're unfamiliar with the breed, we're the ones whose brains were wired by non-union electricians, resulting in us doing things in reverse, getting lost in intersections, feeling like a cat on a screen door when called on in class. Being naturally stoned, in other words. You probably saw me the other day, angling across four lanes of freeway traffic in a desperate attempt to reach the ramp because I mistook the direction of the exit arrow. None of the pieces herein address this issue directly (dyslexia, that is, not my driving), but you may detect a certain pattern of backward logic as you go along. You have my sympathy. Life with dyslexia is basically a matter of seeing things through a smashed windshield; hopefully, not because you misjudged proximity to a semi-trailer while trying for that exit. With luck, I've played the spider more than the fly with this particular web of cracks.

There's a tendency to regard the suburbs, especially outer-ring suburbs such as mine, as blandness personified, a leafy green buffer between the agitation of the city and the rough but pristine countryside. A place where people migrate to get cheaper car insurance, getting loaded means filling the mini-van with groceries, and ethnic awareness is limited to coach boy statues next to the picket fence. Interfaces are seldom that simple. Those pickets can corral some spicy things, though usually not the ATV that rides through them when you're not home. If the 'burbs are a salad, they're arugala.

Toss at will.

CASTLE
BESIEGED

Life's a Birch

For anyone who's interested, Marsha and I are running a blue light special on birch logs at our home.

I should hasten to add that we don't own a tree farm or pulp mill, nor are we enamored of scorched earth policies. We merely live in a house surrounded by borer-friendly foliage. The previous resident, possibly anticipating retirement to the Sonoran Desert, selected specimens with a shelf life shorter than bologna. Result: our yard daily grows more suitable for jack rabbits.

The birches were what originally caught our eye, or hers, anyway. Marsha has a fondness for paper birches stemming from the behemoth in her parents' front yard. Her reaction on first seeing the half-dozen peeling *betula* during a drive-by resulted in a minor case of whiplash. The house might have been sided with corrugated tin, a puddle of raw sewage on the doorstep, and she'd still have bid on it.

I was more skeptical. Even if you're partial to chemicals—which I'm not—caring for paper birches is like paying taxes: maximum investment for minimum return. You can turn your yard into a toxic waste dump with pesticides and still lose the damned things. Over five decades my in-laws have applied the equivalent of the Bhopal spill to their elephantine treasure, and it still looks like it needs Rogaine, the crown nearly devoid of leaves.

Nevertheless, as newlyweds heavily into compromising positions, we agreed to disagree. We bought the birches, er, house, and agreed to avoid toxins for as long as possible. With chin held high we strolled in the gloaming. Our children would thank us and nature, too, in its way.

As it turned out, nature thanked us as children often do, with middle finger extended. Birch #1, situated focally in front, fizzled faster than a sparkler, its trunk riddled with borer holes. We could almost hear it drying up, shup! like a basin emptying, as we lay in bed at night. Birch #2, over our back porch, started losing branches. Wasps the size of F16s hemstitched its girth in search of grubs, divebombing us as we walked by. The remaining four showed signs of wilting.

Obviously, this wasn't the way to go.

There are some pretty lethal poisons out there. Dysistene, for example, is guaranteed to turn you into grub food if inhaled, recreationally or otherwise. According to its label, which takes longer to read than Russian novels, it's toxic to fish, wildlife, birds, and bosses into whose brownies it's baked. You sprinkle it around the dripline and wait for the mushroom cloud to form. Not exactly a product endorsed by Greenpeace.

But better one strong dose than many weaker ones, we reasoned. So, attired as if for a space launch, I dutifully dusted the granules and watered them in. In the process I shed ten pounds through dehydration and got asked by the mailman if I capped oil wells for a living. Measures this extreme would have to bring results!

As it turned out, Dysistene did indeed have a half-life: half of two birches croaked. One of them now resembled a giant cat litter scoop. Nice for Claes Oldenbourg, maybe, but not our idea of horticulture.

In desperation we consulted some nurserymen. Their suggestions were as follows: (1) Continue dousing with pesticides till our yard glowed in the dark. This might not control borers, but would eliminate the need for outdoor lighting. (2) Whack off all the birches knee-high. The new growth, we were told, would prove borer-resistant. Unfortunately, we'd be collecting Social Security before we had shade again. And the aesthetic appeal of truncated trees, especially in winter, is limited.

Quite frankly, at this point we're, er, stumped. We really don't know how to control the borers. We'd like to plant perennial gardens around them, but landscaping around trees that may be burning in the stove next winter is sort of like pushing mutual funds in a nursing home. Maybe we should just enjoy them for as long as we can. After all, we do have other trees in our yard.

Elm trees, for instance.

Creature Discomforts

One aspect of living in a rural suburb is that you get to experience wildlife in all its diversity up close and personal. Very personal. Following is a list of our encounters so far.

1. Chipmunks tunneling under shrubs.
2. Voles tunneling in lawn.
3. Raccoons dumping in flowerboxes and on roof.
4. Carpenter bees boring into soffit.
5. Woodpeckers perforating siding.
6. Yellow jackets nesting in mailbox and bird feeder.
7. Squirrel emptying bird feeder.
8. Groundhog and skunk living under porch.
9. Possum tearing porch screen.
10. Chicken turning over mulch.
11. Deer eating yarrow and ornamental grasses.

The first thing you may notice about this list is that it's a litany of destruction. Nothing on it is calculated to improve property value or quality of life. Quite the opposite. In fact, if all these behaviors had been visited on us at once, we'd now probably be living in a gated community where animals gain entrance only in styrofoam meat trays.

In an age of urban sprawl people tend to assume that all animal encounters that don't take place on the veldt are benign. Actually, there's quite a bit of wiggle room between Pet Doktor and *Animal Planet.* Just because a squirrel shows up on your patio every day for a matzoh cracker doesn't mean he wants to celebrate the seder.

The second, and eerier, thing is that the behaviors seem linked, as though the critters were taking a cue from each other. Kind of like a chain letter from nature saying, 'Screw you.' I'm not into animal conspiracy theories, but it makes you wonder.

I don't go to bed at night with a .22 tucked in my pj's in case a possum tries to ice me, but I also recall Hitchcock's film *The Birds.* As Sir Alfred himself said in an interview, 'The birds had been shot at . . . *eaten* . . .' To my knowledge, no one in our family fights over squirrel's brains, but still: could Timmy Tiptoes be paying us back for all the building in his neighborhood?

More logically, our property invites feral activity for a couple of very good reasons: we're the only house on the block with cedar siding and a woods. This gets us an automatic five-star from Conde Naste Creatures, providing both bed and board for local fauna. Points for taste: these features grabbed *us.* Little did we think we'd become a playground for things without opposable thumbs.

Like all animal encounters, ours ultimately open another window on human experience. Fishermen and hunters swap stories; beleaguered homeowners get to meet hardware store personnel, county extension agents, and mountain men with traps. The latter, especially, carry a *Warning* label.

At first we debated whether having people like Bob on our property posed a bigger health hazard than roof shingles laden with raccoon excrement. But he had a good track record—'Raccoons put my daughter through college,' he said—meaning, he got paid in cash—so we let him do his thing. You could usually tell when he was coming to check the trap when the wind was from his direction. He caught two young females, then the real culprit: a large male which flipped the trap and shredded our grill cover. It was hard to feel sorry for him until, as he was being trucked away, I thought I saw him go cross-eyed. Must have caught a whiff of Bob.

What we really need is another bird of prey like the kestrel that showed up on our feeder last year. Within days it achieved what mothballs, cages, stamping, waving, and hollering ourselves hoarse failed to accomplish: a near-total cessation of varmint activity. Gone, drooping viburna, punctured siding and lumpy lawn. We felt like offering to sharpen its beak on our grinder. Then it disappeared and the legions returned. It may be time for more creative thinking, like having Bob do an occasional drive-by with his windows down. I'll check the by-laws.

Box Unpopular

To celebrate the arrival of kudzu in New England—it was spotted in an alley behind a health food store in New Haven not long ago—I'm conducting my own biological experiment. I'm trying to turn raccoons into porcupines.

The procedure is simple. I've planted prickly pear cactus in all our flower boxes, outside several upstairs windows, to discourage the masked creatures from parking their fannies on them.

This experiment grew out of owning a cedar-sided house. Some diplomatic advice about cedar homes: don't buy one.

Don't misunderstand me. There's nothing wrong with cedar homes per se. They're distinctive to look at and relatively maintenance-free. The problem is that their rustic character encourages you to do cutesy things like planting English perennials that fry in hot weather and adding window boxes that require more attention than a herd of Cheviots. Better to stick with more conventional housing and buy a border collie.

When we put up the boxes not long after moving in, they came under the heading of 'home improvement'—something that makes your house more pleasant to live in and adds to its value. Which shows just how much fantasy and reality can diverge. Far

from adding a chalet-like touch, they've been decadent to the point of outdoor plumbing (more on this later). Being so exposed to the elements, they tend to incur:

(1) Moss (spring and fall). With a few stones and some tiny decorative lanterns we'd have aerial Zen gardens.

(2) Peeling paint (year-round). Cosmetic surgeons must have studied these boxes for the laser peel. They're flakier than Courtney Love, and being precariously situated, tend to discourage touching-up.

In fact, the degree to which our Alpinesque vision neglected vertigo still astounds us. The soil in these boxes, we soon learned, dries out very quickly. Flowers planted in it should be spritzed daily to survive. Ideally, by climbing on the roof with a watering can.

Yeah, right. Did I mention our roof has a slope right out of *Vertical Limits?* Or that the ladder must be positioned even more acutely to clear the shrubs and perennials below? You get the idea.

So we tried more creative (i. e., chicken) irrigation methods, such as dousing the plants with a long-handled window washing brush. This proved useful in rinsing off dirt splashed onto windows and screens. Balancing it so as not to drench ourselves, however, though highly aerobic, made us feel like the Flying Wallendas.

Needless to say, our irrigation resolve waned every year to where we had dried flower arrangements by midsummer. And that was before the raccoons showed up.

Two years ago we started hearing all sorts of footsteps on our roof, accompanied by piles of the proverbial between the fizzled geraniums and vincas on high. Squirrels? Cats?

No, raccoons, a neighbor said. Mature coons evidently like to frequent the same spot for latrine duty. With trees at every corner providing access, our house may as well have had COON COMMODE stenciled on it.

Adding insult to injury, they'd been feasting on grain from our bird feeders, so maize lusher than our lawn now was sprouting outside our windows. *We* couldn't grow squat up there, but the squatting raccoons, depositing fertilizer and seed like seasoned horticulturists, could.

Trapping several of them helped. But this spring there was so much activity aloft we expected them to rap on the skylight for Charmin. By June the boxes were rank as a pasture. We'd had it. Heidi never had to deal with this. And goats, unlike raccoons, give milk.

But before I could reach for a crowbar . . .

While pruning a rose bush one day, and losing a fair amount of blood in the process, a thorn stuck in my brain.

'Cactus?' the man at the greenhouse said. 'Sure; I've got a few around back.' I asked him what sort of care they required. He looked at me like I'd wandered in out of the desert myself. 'Oh, they just sit there, basically, and once in a while I repot them.'

Sold.

I've never been through basic training, but slithering up a ladder and roof in bulky sweaters and welding gloves with flats of prickly pear—which must be the heaviest plants for their size on record—then balancing those flats with one hand as you plant while trying not to slide off the roof into a juniper bush, I suspect, comes close.

But now they're in, and alive—I think. With the fall chill the cacti look like wrinkled Mickey Mouse ears. Next spring, I'm told, they'll sprout little yellow flowers. I've noticed a little dirt scratched up around them, but that's it. The raccoons may prefer the compost heap from now on.

Together Weather

Every so often a citizen of northeast Ohio, presumably wishing to test the mettle just acquired in an empowerment course, will write a letter to the *Cleveland Plain Dealer* criticizing our climate. Readers immediately respond with enough vitriol to reignite that much-maligned watercourse, the Cuyahoga, and for good measure set afire all others within a fifty mile radius.

As they say in mob pictures, never take sides against the family. And weather is very much a family issue here. Along with other regionally endemic flaws such as our dangerously curvaceous innerbelt and waistlines, our smoking habits, our sports teams that continually throttle themselves in the last minute, it unites us against outsiders' guff. Lacking a cultural mensch to give our foibles a positive spin the way John Waters does for Baltimore's, we deal severely with those who break faith, either with verbal vigilantism or the Jewish mafia version of the necklace murder: we put a bagel around your neck and set fire to it. The reason Art Modell still has ears is because they're flame retardant.

Not that our climate couldn't give a camel an extra hump, as the saying goes. Mother Nature's on Midol here 24/7, and could use a prescription for lithium, too. The average wind speed in Chicago, America's Windy City, is 10 mph. Cleveland's is 11, and not just near Slyman's Deli. Summers are so clammy you wring out your underwear *before* it's washed; winters, the sun disappears behind a 300 foot ceiling like a pizza delivery guy with your change. Monsoon and drought play tag all year long. The transitional seasons can be tough to catch without a strobe.

But like true family, we know how to survive. To escape the heat we bribe the neighbor with a case of Bud to use his kiddie pool, or head for an open spot in Lake Erie's algae. In cold weather we either flock to Florida, preferring a spell of Aunt Rose's nattering in the polyester pant capital of the world to one more Alberta Clipper forecast, or hibernate, leaving the den only to forage for breadsticks, videos, and pharmacopoeia, and to take Lamaze classes to prep for all those babies conceived during rewind.

And just as families carp about the nephew who likes stealing boxcars of Levis but continue to scrounge his bail, we take perverse pride in our weather privations. If the climate in San Diego is a well-oiled J. Lo in a bikini, around here it's Elvin Bishop's *Sweet Potato:* cross-eyed, lumpy, with fake hair, trailing gin bottles everywhere. But you love her just the same, or at least share the same bar tab. Driving on Route 2 in mid-February, with wind-whipped Lake Erie chop barely visible through your slush-spattered windshield, drizzle from the soiled clouds just above your car roof turning the sooty snow even darker, you can't help feeling proud. Who the hell else has weather this bad? you think, as you hit a puddle that sends you careening into a guardrail.

One aspect of the local weather scene, however, even the convention bureau has trouble sugarcoating: lake effect snow. This occurs in only a handful of places on earth, presumably where some grave offense against natural law occurred, such as putting a lime wedge in a brewski. For people not from Cleveland, Buffalo, Syracuse, and the eastern shore of the Black Sea, and moose not living near Great Slave Lake, lake effect snow happens when clouds pass over a large body of water that hasn't yet frozen over, draw moisture from it, and when next encountering land, which has cooled more rapidly, dump it all as snow within a two block area.

If you think I'm kidding, you should see the faces of west side Clevelanders downtown the day after a lake effect storm. You can almost hear the *Twilight Zone* theme playing as they gawk at cars from the snow belt. Being less geographically depraved (i.e., to windward), the only thing white on their cars is bird poop, while east side cars resemble oversized cupcakes.

Lake effect is like a *Ziggie* cartoon: one day you're outside with the kids burying the Shelty in leaves, the next you're trying to find your garage. Because it's so wet, lake effect snow weighs about as much as tungsten, so it does a lot of damage. Mailboxes get smacked over by crescents of plowed glop, power lines and trees come down, roofs cave in, schools and businesses close. People who haven't run since grade school scoot up and down the street like Mo Greene flagging trucks to clear their driveway. It's like an enormous wet diaper descends on you. The only thing good about it, other than getting to break in your new snow blower, is that it keeps Aunt Rose from reciprocating your visit. Families need a break from each other, and that ain't taking sides.

Lightning-Up

J ust when you think current events have jaded you to the point
of narcolepsy, one comes along that really gives you a jolt.
When the current is several thousand volts and fries appliances
in your home, it's even more compelling.

A recent Sunday found the three of us together at the din-
ing table eating, an event about as frequent as the appearance of
Halley's comet. It was one of those November evenings, with tor-
rents of rain and continuous vollies of thunder and lightning, that
inspire gothic novelists and sump pump manufacturers. We're
on a slab, though, which left us free to attack Marsha's salmon;
even persnickety Anna took her eyes off *Lizzie McGuire* once in
a while for a bite.

As they say, if it sounds too good to be true, it probably is.
Midway through the first fillet our back yard blew up. There was
a burst of light like a Julia Roberts closeup on widescreen, followed by an explosion that left our ears ringing. Lights flashed,
then went off; ditto TVs, phones, computer. Blinded, deafened,
plunged into darkness, all in the space of five seconds.

My first impulse was to start reading.

(If that's not exactly normative in such situations, thank my dad. That was how he handled emergencies, especially storm-related ones. Our car slides in the ditch outside our house during a blizzard? No problem. Go to bed and crack open the latest issue of *American Artist*. The windows in our rented cabin leak, turning the adjacent floor into a wading pool? No sweat. Put your feet up on a table and remain absorbed in Lawrence Welk's memoirs. Maybe he was trying to teach me that panic makes poor decisions. Presumably, had the American public taken this approach and headed for the libraries instead of the banks after Black Thursday, we could have avoided the Depression.)

Unfortunately, as we'd now been reduced to candlepower, and Anna was already experiencing telewithdrawal—a foaming at the mouth coupled with periodic yelps of *'Hey Arnold!!'*, requiring immediate attention—I had to postpone my education in favor of a flashlight. The breaker brought some of the lights back on, then we cell- phoned the fire department and electric company, and waited—-Marsha, inside, to shield the salmon from our cats; myself, outside.

Funny, how one minute you can be enjoying a Currier and Ives moment, the next be standing at the foot of your driveway in a downpour, in the dark, under your kid's kitty-ear umbrella (because it has a plastic tip), waiting to flag a fire truck.

And that's about it, folks. No harrowing tales of people with foggers quenching sparking circuitry, or spending the night in a Days Inn. As with most catastrophes, the excitement ended in seconds, leaving only insurance bean-counters to deal with and a game show-like trip to *Best Buy* to replace electronica. The VFDs even wiped their wellies before entering.

The most interesting thing about the whole business, in fact, may have been how little interest it actually stirred up in the community. A snippet appeared in the local paper, but didn't identify our house, so there was no parade of gawkers the next day. One neighbor called; another, aware that a stray chicken hung around our back yard, asked if we were opening a KFC franchise. (Guess who gets an anonymous dirty valentine next year?) Otherwise, it was business as usual in our development. As yet, we haven't noticed Anna's sitter wearing rubber beach sandals around our house or the UPS driver genuflecting when he delivers.

We couldn't even get anecdotal mileage out of the hit. Subsequent conversations made it clear that unless lightning actually singes your eyebrows, you don't even make the cut for global misfortune. Everyone knows someone it's happened to *worse*. 'My son in Atlanta lost seven TVs to lightning,' said one acquaintance. He now plays in a band called Surge Overkill, presumably.

But that's okay. What we lost in fame we gained in perspective, thereby numbing the temporary shock of blown appliances and higher homeowner's premiums. Our lightning strike now seems like a dream.

Well, almost. There's still a burn mark in our TV cabinet where the lightning grounded. It looks a bit like a marijuana leaf. Makes you wonder who's lobbying for NORML these days.

Saleing, Saleing

Marsha and I just spent an evening tagging stuff for our garage sale next weekend. In years past, garage sales made me uneasy. I've gotten over that.

They now fill me with terror.

The history of garage sales should read like the bedtime story Calvin's dad read him in an old *Calvin and Hobbes* strip: 'Once upon a time there was a little boy who needed to go to sleep. The end.'

Unfortunately, I'm no salesman. As with rugby, politics, and open heart surgery, with sales you've got to enjoy getting down and dirty, really wallow in the blood and mud, to succeed. I wallow poorly. It comes from not being allowed to play in the rain as a kid. I couldn't go near a puddle without Mom hurling soap at me. I was the only kid on the block with a bathtub ring in my driveway.

For one thing, I bargain about as well as a state trooper. I figure, if it's in good shape and the price is fair, why stand gassing about it? This is decidedly at odds with the garage sale ethos, of which there are several aspects:

(1) There is no relation between a customer's net worth and an item's price. You can count on the driver of a

20

$40000 crewcab dually 4 x 4 with detailing and bug
shield to pull up, examine the wrench set priced at $3
(which originally cost $50) and promptly offer half that.

You: Well, sir, considering it was owned by the
Duchess of Cornwall and insured by Lloyd's of London,
I was kinda hopin' for at least $2.50.

He (adjusting Oakleys): Nah, too much.

You: Tell you what: for $2.25 I'll gladly rotate your
tires and lick your running boards clean.

He: Sounds good. I've also got this zit on my back I
can't reach . . .

(2) As hinted, blue book values do not apply here. Even
brand-new items will be treated like landfill substrata. I
recently sold a commercial riding mower with more
new components than Cher, the closest thing to a top
fuel dragster in lawn care. This thing will climb trees
with the right octane. From the offers I received, you'd
have thought I was pushing an ox cart, minus the ox. I
practically sued prospective buyers for defamation of
character. The guy who finally bought it paid the asking
price as long as I agreed to bring him breakfast in bed
for three years if it ever failed.

Which brings up another crucial point of garage sale dy-
namics: guarantees.

People who shop at garage sales remind me of that fishing
camp story about the old squaw who sat on her cabin porch all
day, toothless, unwashed, and dribbling tobacco juice down her
chin. When asked why he kept her around, the owner said, 'Boys,
when she starts to look good to you, it's time to go home.'

The difference here is that, unlike fishermen, the buyer will be departing with the squaw and still expecting her to deliver like Foxy Brown when he gets home. You may be in Chapter 11, owing money in 12 states, and he will still expect a lifetime guarantee, especially when he shows up again the next day with his trash-talking spouse.

She: That toaster oven you sold Merle: it ain't workin'.

You: It worked yesterday. He plugged it in over there!

She: Yeah, but that's *your* electricity!

I have no stomach for this jive.

Unfortunately, Marsha and I have no choice in the matter. We absolutely, positively must have a garage sale at least every other year, or sleep in the tool shed. Because the previous owner and builder of our house had fewer possessions than Gandhi, he absolutely, positively did not believe in storage space. A lunchbox has more storage than our house. This is especially troublesome if you have a growing child with doting grandparents who believe her living space should resemble F. A. O. Schwarz.

Most of the stuff in this year's sale, in fact, is Anna's, including the specialty items that provide its theme. Every sale should have a theme. It makes you think you're mounting a Broadway show rather than cleaning a stable. Our theme this year is Things We Amputated Toes On. They include baby gates we didn't quite hurdle, a stroller I never got the hang of folding, especially in flip-flops, and an expensive, Japanese-made high chair whose legs reach from our kitchen to Okinawa. Stuff like that makes garage sales seem healthy.

I better start learning to wallow.

No Basement, No Bargain

When my mother was in grade school, long before Betty Spaghetty, she wanted one thing more than anything else in the world: buck teeth. She achieved this to some degree by pushing against the back of her incisors with the ball of her thumb as she sat at her desk every day.

I'm wondering if similar persistence could get my family a basement. If all of us (and maybe the cats, if we gave them mahi-mahi every morning) jumped in place downstairs in unison long enough we might eventually create a divot deep enough for storage.

They say when buying a house it's wise to get more space than you need, just in case you wake up one morning with septuplets and your unemployed brother-in-law with the three schnauzers comes to live with you and you decide to start collecting old toilet tank lids to sculpt with. What 'they' mean is, with a basement. Never mind the extra bedroom; there are such things as bunk beds, and that half bath is apt to collect dust unless you're having an affair. With a basement, even a moldy, armadillo bug-ridden one, you're free to become the klepto you were meant to be.

I used to laugh at people who fixated on certain features when house hunting. Like the single guy I knew with one car who absolutely had to have a place with three garages. He could have bought a *ger* in Mongolia and been happy as long as it had an attached three car garage. What a doofus, I thought. Now, this guy seems like a genius. If we woke up one morning with a three car garage, not to mention a basement, our next vacation would be in Mecca by way of Lourdes.

If I had to do high school over again—in other words, if hell really did exist—I'd pay more attention in geometry, so I'd know what to do if I ever lived in a house where I spent all my free time stacking and fitting and condensing. Life without a basement isn't so much a bowl of cherries as trying to fit a watermelon into a mason jar.

You'd think life on a slab would be very efficient. That without the option of storing Aunt Harriet's hutch while she's doing missionary work your life would be free from clutter. That may be true in traffic areas, where the excruciating pain of stubbed toes is apt to discourage hitting estate sales. But as storage areas become jammed you find yourself feeling more and more like a Sherpa as you try to get at stuff. A curious hierarchy of availability develops, with seldom-used things migrating to the topmost shelf of a cupboard or the furthest attic corner. Utimately you may find it less stressful to convince your spouse to go on a cruise than get at her sleeping bag for a trip to the lake.

And though memorabilia may be assembled airtight as a country club, for some reason the way things are boxed actually gets more haphazard as space diminishes. Stuff formerly crated separately as 1st GRADE, 2nd GRADE, etc., now gets lumped together as SCHOOL CRAP, so that you need an entire weekend to find your spelling bee medal.

No Basement, No Bargain

When you're stumped for storage, especially if you have small fry, occasions such as birthdays and Christmas, with their prospect of truckloads of new merchandise, acquire a positively menacing aspect. You see them coming the way a hobbled wildebeest watches an approaching pride of lions, knowing you'll be swallowed shortly. Try as you might to discourage an obsession with material things, kids' appetite for them not only grows along with them but inclines toward the gigantic. No more doll furniture to avoid while vacuuming; now it's a scale-model department store. Your primary concern is no longer whether you can afford it but whether it comes with a hook to hang it from the ceiling.

The upside of having no space is that you have marketable warehousing skills to teach your brother-in-law so he can stay in his own place. And that's even before you trade your second car for a forklift.

FAITH IN GRAVITY: PARENTS

Knock First, Then Leave

I see in the paper where a Japanese computer team has calculated the value of *pi* to 1.24 trillion places. What a coincidence. This is the approximate number of times in fourteen years of marriage my in-laws have shown up at my house unexpectedly.

I get the feeling both sequences will continue *ad infinitum.*

If you're saddled with more dire in-law issues, such as trying to talk them out of breeding mastiffs in their basement, what follows will seem rather trivial. 'People should have such problems,' my wife says. And she's right. They *should* have them, so they can see what it's like to have a rugby team show up on your doorstep just as you're changing the cat boxes.

Full disclosure: I get along okay with Marsha's parents. It's not like they have mob connections and bring around bodies to feed the In-Sinkerator. But their philosophy of visitation derives from that old FedEx commercial: despite repeated requests, they absolutely, positively refuse to call ahead. The most warning we've ever had from them was when their van backfired in our driveway.

As you may infer, I'm not used to people dropping in. I grew up rather isolated, to the point where you'd have thought a large 'X' was painted on our door to signify the plague. My father hit

70 when I graduated from high school, so most people he knew either were too decrepit or too dead to travel. My mother's family lived overseas, in England, but her craving for privacy made me suspect we'd have seen as much of them if they'd lived next door. I was forever untangling the mail-man from the barbed wire she festooned on our porch. At Christmas, Santa made sure to bring his passport with him when he came down the chimney.

So I'm just not used to people showing up at my house, especially via air drop. But it's more than the unexpected sight of in-laws waving and yelling, as though they'd returned from a stint in Uruguay, that unnerves me; it's the embarrassed memories it awakens.

Unlike my mother, my dad was a gregarious person who liked to visit people outside the funeral home. Unfortunately, like my in-laws, he made a vocation of catching them unawares.

Armed with a yellowed scrap of paper on which he'd scrawled the address (never the phone number) of an office buddy who'd retired during the Roosevelt administration (Theodore, that is), he'd launch us into the blue ether of a Saturday morning. Millennia later, with gas tank and bellies on Empty and bladders Full, we'd arrive at some backwater abode to discover one of two things: (1) Dad's friend now resided in a nearby cemetery; (2) Dad's friend and/or spouse sitting down to a robust meal of Metamucil and prunes.

It made for awkward conversation.

Once, we showed up at the farm of a shirttail relative, miles from anywhere, after dark, and found no one home. An hour later she returned to find us sitting next to the barn in our car like hit men, watching moths strafe a pole lamp. Thankfully, she wasn't an NRA member. 'I could just spank all of you,' she said.

It's doubtful my rear would have been redder than my face at that point.

It complicates things that my extended family operate in a different time zone than we do. We run on Eastern Standard, they're on Rocky Mountain—another reason Marsha and I have formally postponed foreplay till retirement. It's hard enough to indulge in preliminaries with children around, let alone with grandma and grandpa yodeling under our window. That's too much like high school. Especially as they have a key.

I still can't believe I agreed to it. 'I don't want my parents to feel like this is Fort Knox,' said Marsha. 'With our income, that'll never happen,' I tried to reassure her. But no. They need to get a change of clothes for Anna, etc. So I let the drain plug on our moat be pulled. In the space of one lifetime I went from being raised in a castle from which boiling pitch was poured onto visitors to living in a restroom.

My own, that is. I spend a lot more time up there these days, reading, mostly. I've even redecorated it. My in-laws think it's my diet.

Why I Don't Skydive

If I've learned anything at all in life, it's that you can learn an awful lot by observing people through the looking glass—by watching them behave in ways that counter the preferred. At times, it's enough to send you tumbling down a rabbit hole.

In a mall once, at a safe distance, I witnessed the following hare-raising scene. A boy's father refused to indulge him in a snack as the two of them were leaving the building. Deaf to his son's anguished wails, he simply walked out the door. The youngster had an immediate neurological meltdown. Face shriveling red like a rotten tomato, legs and arms stiffening, he started jolting into the air at every step like a crazed marionette as he trailed his dad outside. He continued this rickety mania across the parking lot, almost vaulting cars as he went. After that I never again threw a tantrum in public. I was 24 by then, anyway.

It was the same with sport fishing, about which my father taught me everything he knew, i.e., nothing. Consequently I now have not only fair knowledge of the subject but the highest regard for our finny friends and their environment.

His method was simple: by pursuing our piscatorial quarry as if to chase them away, he leveled the playing field, thus implying they deserved respect. He did this in a number of ways.

A common rap against modern sportsmen is that they overmatch their game. That their sophisticated gear eliminates any chance of prey escaping.

Not so with Dad. He made every effort to ensure that perishable components in our tackle were never replaced and thus bound to fail under stress. His by-laws stated that our line, normally strong enough to tame a thrashing muskellunge, should be sufficiently rotten to liberate a sunfish. Likewise, that the mesh of our landing net should allow trapped fish a speedy exit. One evening a pike the size of a canoe paddle zoomed out the cords so fast Dad fell backward into an open tackle box. It took an hour to disimpale him, by which time the only things biting were mosquitoes.

This leads to a second aspect of Dad's reductive approach: strategy. Afloat, he made sure we spent as little time fishing as possible, usually by trolling with our outboard motor. In theory this should have presented our lures to schools of fish but in reality created bird's nests of line around the propeller which required half a day to untangle. Occasionally we tried drift fishing. Fish, like realtors, hang out in rocks and weeds where prey congregates. This was Dad's cue to linger in the middle of the lake over an unsullied sand bottom in water so clear every pisces for miles, with or without prescription lenses, could see (and avoid) us.

But the audio dimension showcased Dad's conservationist ethic. Sound travels twice as fast underwater as in air, which is why fish never buy stereos. It's also the reason normally peaceable anglers make seagull-like gestures at friendly water skiers.

Why I Don't Skydive

Dad didn't need to. Perhaps his German ancestry made him fond of metal. Homage to Krupp, or 'blood and iron.' Everything in our arsenal had to resonate: aluminum boat and bait bucket, steel tackle boxes, rods, and helmsman's seat. We were a floating drumkit, cued by Dad's fishing attire, which included cuffed pants dating to V-E day, with legs wide as a purse seine. Trolled behind the boat, they'd have scoured the lake. Instead, they merely caught *on* things. No gazelle on dry land, my father became a hobbled elephant afloat, upsetting everything. Bony-assed as he was, he kept moving around to get comfortable. As did the fish. Around us.

Ironically, Dad's unwittingly 'cricket' ways afloat actually led to a compromise in principle; in other words, success.

Historically, women have been unwelcome aboard ship, considered a jinx, and for good reason: men know that broads aboard will outclass them, and with less effort, relegating male egos, like rats, to the hold.

Dad, of course, was blissfully unaware of this. To give my mother a break from cooking leftover baitfish, he started bringing her along on our finny forays. He reasoned that a homemaker seated in the bow with scarf knotted around hair and line looped around a toe, reading a paperback, would threaten neither self-esteem nor the fish population.

His logic was impeccably flawed. Mom's presence actually weighted the odds heavily in our favor. So heavily, that the boat began to nose dive from the fish that kept accumulating at her feet.

Though Mom's success alarmed him at first, Dad soon adjusted: he gave up fishing altogether, the crowning glory of his sportsmanship. No longer pursued by us, the fish got back to chasing each other.

Sounds ecological to me.

'Worse Where There's None'

Should the stock market continue eddying like the Niagara whirlpool, I know at least one person who won't be sucked down. She's been living pretty austerely since coming to the States in 1947. Prior to that she endured eight years of rationing in England. She's used to making-do. Not only that, she can't help it.

Mom has never adjusted to living in a culture of plenty. American abundance has always been suspect for her, as though it might vaporize any second in the flash of a doodle bug. She still walks, as it were, on the shards of a shattered world.

This is both sad and amusing. You'd like to see someone who's been through the mill gain more than crumbs for her efforts. When the loaf is there but she continues only pecking at it, head-scratching is in order. Though Mom's antics haven't yet reached the point of hanging toilet paper out to dry, they may eventually lead me to a dermatologist.

Most of us, for instance, like to do a job as expeditiously as possible—sometimes, even when we're working for someone else—while using the proper tools, so we can get back to PlayStation and studying Old Norse. Or we delegate it. This is known as maximizing your time while saving yourself to fight another day.

Mom takes the opposite tack. She believes that work is basically self-obliteration, and if the job takes ten years to finish, so much the better. Every small stone must contain a mountain. This is expressed in the following principles:

(1) Technology more recent than Neolithic is suspect. (This is the same race, mind, that gave us penicillin and the aircraft carrier.)

(2) One should never call for help unless pinned beneath rubble.

(3) Gibbering insanity is the ultimate job satisfaction.

These criteria have produced some memorable penal-style projects. Such as the time she paneled the basement using an eight-inch pruning saw. (No exaggeration.) Or broke up a cement laundry tub with a hammer and screwdriver. You won't see her on *This Old House* anytime soon.

But Stone Age rehab is just the beginning of Mom's taste for domestic Outward Bound experience. As a form of ritual purification, what beats turning your living space into a combination ice house/sweat lodge?

For a variety of reasons—leisurely health care, antique housing, more T-cells from drinking tea—the British have a higher threshold of bodily discomfort than we do. Mom herself was raised in a row house with coal-burning fireplaces. After resisting the Hun she wasn't about to capitulate to a thermostat.

This had severe ramifications in northeast Ohio. In winter it meant sides of beef could be hung in our living room without spoiling. In summer, even after we acquired a window unit, it denoted something called the Lovely Cool Breeze, essentially a Zen meteorological concept which did and didn't exist. Usually invoked at my request to turn on the a.c., it referred to occasional puffs of humidity-laden hot air in our back yard. Throwing open the patio door, Mom would point to a couple of quivering leaves, as though discerning a new ring around Saturn, and raptly exclaim deliverance was at hand. Meanwhile, I crawled gasping toward our tiny oscillating fan. The English, I suspect, didn't go to the desert just because it was clean.

Sometimes this propensity for primitivism makes for irony, as in matters of attire. Mom's taste for retro enables her to cut a decidedly youthful figure.

I am an only child. Instead of becoming hand-me-downs, my stuff got passed *up* as soon as she and I became the same height. Back when Nixon was not a crook, she started latching onto gym tees, flannel shirts, and baseball caps the minute I outgrew or got sick of them. 'Plenty of wear left,' she'd say, and says, though some of those garments now contain more air than fabric.

Closing in on eighty, Mom is entitled to wear any hue in the rainbow, or even button-down flares, if she wants. Nevertheless, it's unnerving to go around and find her looking like a roadie for the Foo Fighters—a Cubist image of myself, thirty years ago. At an age when other women have settled into cardigans she's unwittingly putting her own spin on the geriatric teen myth: grunge grandmother. Maybe it will turn into a career for her: Gen Y fashion guru. After all, Grandma Moses took up painting at the same age.

Just don't expect her to get comfortable with it.

THE POUNDING ON THE STAIR: PARENTING

The Ounce
That May Prevent

Once upon a time, in a flood of rheuminess triggered by too many tearjerker videos, Marsha and I decided to try for a baby. We did all the things that normally accompany such notions.

We consigned prophylactics to the back of the medicine cupboard, where they gathered dust with *The Joy of Sex*. I learned that a basal thermometer is not used to cook pesto sauce, and bought boxer shorts to keep my gonads cool. Marsha consulted her horoscope and read novels after the deed with her knees in the air like a grasshopper's. Months later, her belly waxed great— with Hershey bars ingested in despair at not being pregnant. 'What's wrong with us?' she wailed, snorting a Mr. Goodbar.

Around us, friends and family generated offspring with alarming frequency. Our conversations took a punitive turn, ranging from 'Why us?' to 'Why not us?' When we started watching the apes barf at the zoo, pretending it was morning sickness, we decided I should be checked out. The following suggestions may help men similarly inclined.

Cousin to Secretariat

Right off the fungo bat, let me assure you there's nothing shameful about semenalysis. This isn't a moral issue, merely a chance to find out if you have income potential if you lose your job. The status and dimension of your privates is not being questioned. You can be the size of Rasputin and be sterile, and you've heard the one about acorns. You may even get a vicarious thrill from knowing that someone like Beaker in *The Muppets* is scrutinizing your sperm.

Uncle Wiggly Goes to Mednet

Initially the process couldn't be simpler. The nice doctor will ask you a few subtle questions, such as, 'Have you ever been kicked in the groin by a horse?', then dispatch you to the desk for instructions. You'll be handed a paper bag containing a plastic jar and a sheet with the phone number of the lab and the nearest adult video store. At this point you may wish to dispel the tension with a casually witty remark, such as, 'Can I check myself for a hernia at the same time?' This will establish rapport with the staff to the point where, as you exit into the crowded waiting room, the nurse known as The Human Air Horn will bellow, '*Remember, no sex for 72 hours beforehand!*'

When the Hallelujah Chorus Starts

The time has come, the walrus said, to time your coming. The appointment's made, the lab anxiously waits to process you.

It's now up to you to show that, though you once made it with Carla beneath roaring high school bleachers in thirty seconds flat, you can now be impotent in the privacy of your home.

Okay, so a jar is no substitute for the queen of the bell lap. But this is one deadline you've got to meet.

So go wild. Discover that expired yogurt in back of the fridge. Dig out that fantasy of Liz Hurley you've been saving for when your wife's horny and you'd rather watch *NFL Total Access*. Have phone sex with defrocked priests. It's for a good cause. And remember, if you don't come through—well, remember John Wayne Bobbitt?

Don't Burp the Tupperware

Remember all the times you made fun of women because they couldn't whip it out in an emergency? That time you sat giggling in the bow when your sister had to use the bait bucket? Or when you threw a dead muskrat in the women's restroom at the class picnic? It's payback time, buddy. You're about to discover several things simultaneously:

(1) hand-eye coordination is useful in more than athletics;
(2) screwtop jars can be more painful than zippers;
(3) that body part you'd forgotten about since seventh grade health class—the one that rhymes with pendulum—is still attached.

You're on your own with this one, dude. Just pretend you're putting a mute on a trombone, and try not to forget the melody.

Hold the Mayo

Now that you've got the goods and staunched the bleeding, it's time to roll. With every passing second a few more fingerlings fry in the shallows. But drive safely; you *don't* want to plead this one in traffic court. And no stopping at fast food restaurants, lest the lab find itself processing a quarter pounder with cheese and you take home ranch dressing. If your donation takes place in winter, keep it inside your coat to insulate it, the way you did with your pet rabbit as a kid.

Just One Kiss Before I Go

That's about it. Write your name on the label the receptionist gives you and stick it on the jar. (Do it inside the bag. Walking down the street with a loaded poop scooper is one thing, waving your bodily fluids around in a lobby quite another.) Tell her the donation was made two minutes ago and see if she doesn't look at your crotch. Call the lab later to see if you can start hanging out with someone named Mario who wears gold chains or need to live on zinc for awhile.

If you're okay, the next step is your spouse's, something called a hysterosalpyngogram, where the ob-gyn scopes her innards. You may be embarking on a costly series of in vitro measures that'll leave her crazy-hormonal, and you impotent after all with worry over paying for them.

Anyone for adoption?

You've Got Male (Martha Stewart, That Is)

One thing about Phyllis Diller: she's consistent. The comic who once claimed she put up her hair in hand grenades and when they went off, it was done, also thinks overdoing housework is bunk. Especially when you have a family.

This sounds like good advice. Years down the road, when your kid brings home that special someone who'll whisk him away to overdraft protection land, you want some memories in place. You don't want to be like Vinnie's parents in the film *Buffalo 66*, with a single snapshot to show of his formative years. What a hoot. Having one picture of your son is a great way to ensure another of him will appear on the post office wall one day.

When Marsha and I adopted Anna, I was determined not to sweat the small stuff. Especially microorganisms. Fortune cookie crumbs on a car seat. Pasta sauce on a shoe. Jam in the diaper bag. I'm not used to epidemics in the making, but it's still healthier for Anna than ingesting lead in the orphanage.

It's not easy, though. As with child-rearing generally, it's impossible to guage the adjustment beforehand. Advice and opinion sometimes verge on ludicrous. One piece I read suggested leaving sticky candy behind the drapes and forgetting about it.

This sounds like a better way to catch armadillo bugs than prepare for child-related disorder.

First-time parents with average junk food habits, already familiar with snacks under the sofa cushions, soon grow accustomed to finding all manner of victuals in varying stages of decay in, around, and behind furniture and appliances. You're not, however, prepared for food that blends with surfaces, especially if your home is furnished in wood tones. Peanut butter, hot cereal, apple juice go perfectly with carpet, bookshelf, counter. Even with two cats exuding all sorts of viscosity, we're still not used to the shock of squishy coolness between toes or leaving patches of skin on something we were leaning on.

Neither do isolated placebos of mess prepare you for the sheer quantity of chaos left by an active child—a table cleared of books and magazines, or a drawer emptied, in a nanosecond; a toy chest or laundry basket upended. Short of holding a demo derby in your living room, nothing will.

There *have* been moments, akin to capping Mt. Etna with chewing gum, when I've tried to impose undue precision on Anna's vision of the world. Take her room—please. Coordinated colors, Marimekko border, precisely placed furniture. And why not? The folly lay in presuming that idealized scheme could extend to her playthings. Books would be aligned, videos alphabetized, dolls in their strollers, rarin' to go. My pride and joy was the window seat. As it filled with stuffed pals of every size, shape, and marketing ploy, I envisioned a tableau of childhood whimsy so perfect it could be the centerfold of *Parents* magazine for generations. Fatherhood hubris personified.

Enter reality. Each day it became harder to buck the tide of my daughter's will, which saw the window seat as a mosh pit instead of art. Try telling a two-year old Elmo should sit behind Arthur because of perspective. Finally, like a salmon in a brackish pool, I turned belly-up. The friends now lie in jumbled disarray like clams on a plate. But if my stint as male Martha Stewart ended prematurely, I take comfort in knowing little hands that make a mess can be schooled to clean it up. That stage, along with potty training, is fast approaching. Be it wastebasket, toybox, or commode, we'll all soon be spending lots of time around receptacles. Phyllis Diller might not approve, but it's either that or borrow some of her hand grenades.

Sleeping With Myself

Like most guys who become dads, I've had the following intimate conversation with my wife: 'Yo, are we ever going to do it again?'

That's how it is. One minute we're cruising, it's there, pretty much; the next, we're chopped liver. On rye. I know for a fact there's a chopped liver school dads attend to learn to put their ego on the back burner, just as landlords attend one to be cheap and deaf. It includes such courses as learning never to finish a sentence, a meal, a bowel movement (*kids* need diapers? Hell.), or a telephone call, and how to watch TV out the back of your head.

Fact: the reason more couples don't get pregnant soon after childbirth has nothing to do with finances, exhaustion or the contraceptive effects of breast feeding. It's because a little body now occupies the gap in the spark plug as effectively as the Hays Code once did on the bigscreen. The first year they're doing crib duty, Mommy's sleeping with the springal, or everyone's in the sack together.

Full disclosure: Marsha and I were spared crib patrol because Anna's adopted. She slept in a crib for fourteen months in the orphanage and for three minutes with us. When we got back from China she took one look at those bars and said, 'What about my Miranda rights?'

The group bed approach is known as the Sears Family bed. Dr. William Sears, that is; it has nothing to do with band saws. We know a couple who practice it with their son. It involves both parents sleeping with their offspring till they're old enough to do trigonometry exercises on their own, or thereabouts. It supposedly results in kinder, gentler children who won't drop an air conditioner on your head as you and your spouse linger on the doorstep watching the sunset.

To me, it seems, er, weird. It brings to mind a relative who did her psych internship in a community where front teeth are optional. Her favorite joke was, Suzy skipped the prom because her dad worked overtime.

Okay, so it's my wife's side of the family.

The little boy in question is three years old and very sweet. He has the sort of round, cherubic face you see on oatmeal boxes. His vocabulary does not include lyrics by Snoop Dogg. The last time we saw him, though, he did mention 'Mommy's bresses.' Gulp.

I recently ran this by my ready reference in matters parental, Colleen. Colleen has three kids, babysits four others out of her home, and her eyebrows match. She has twelve brothers and sisters. She survives kids the way Bill Clinton survived shame.

'Oh, right, and what kind of relationship do Steven's parents have?' she snorted, throwing a rolling block on her son. (Colleen has no patience with hangers-on. Rumor has it she toilet trained her kids in the womb. You can imagine her opinion of a neighbor who breast-feeds her five year old son: 'Whip it out with the Jif when he gets home from kindergarten!')

The Pounding on the Stair: Parenting

I can't tell you if Steven's parents are rewriting the *Kama Sutra*, or whether he will undergo puberty before he spells 'cat,' but at least I'm not worried about Anna asking me to help fasten her brassiere for high school commencement.

My own graduation (from chopped liver school) is still pending. Despite numerous enticements, including the promise never again to roll my eyes and smirk when she salivates over Robert Redford, Marsha continues to sleep with Anna. Any hope of action depends on waking her without disturbing pee-wee, a proposition that would daunt your average cat burglar, partly because our cats are *also* in the bed. A regular brahmacharya bunkhouse. You'd have to be a snake to even make it a Family bed.

There are times, about as often as presidential primaries, when I've made it past creaking floorboards, felines (whom I've considered renaming Sheik and Trojan), and my wife's tendency to waken as though fired from a gun, and tiptoed her back to our conjugal pallet. You know the rest. We've barely cleared for take-off before the air raid siren sounds. *MOMMIEEE!!* Suddenly I'm alone again with a box of Girl Scout cookies.

They say candy is dandy but sex don't rot your teeth. That's why I see my dentist regularly.

Wait Till They're Teenagers (A Primer on Denapping)

About the time Anna decided diapers were kid stuff and no longer rent public air with cries of *peepee!* and *poopoo!*, she also stopped napping. Sort of like Congress passing a bill permitting booze in drinking fountains with an amendment stipulating, Well Liquor Only. The ticker tape parade that accompanied no longer spending half our wages on Huggies and wipes, or being summoned to the changing table in the middle of dessert, quickly turned to a funeral procession.

In the lingo of developmental psychogeography, childhood behavior stages normally are called 'plateaus.' The youngster stays at a certain level till enough Chuck E. Cheese tokens are collected to power him, like a Jeep in a TV ad, up the next escarpment, where he remains till the rebate period is over, and so on. By contrast, the end of napping is more a tableland stretching unbroken to the horizon. Meanwhile . . .

The difference between a normal, active child who's napped and one who hasn't around 5 PM is a bit like Atlanta before and after General Sherman arrived, minus the salting of the earth. A tired and wired youngster doesn't just give you a hard time; he makes you think you're on the set of *Gremlins*.

51

For example, the announcement that dinner is ready, once merely ignored, now inspires an aria of pain usually associated with primitive dentistry, as though you were serving fish eyes in aspic. But meals are a cinch compared with the subject of picking up toys. A minefield before, it now resembles Omaha Beach. We became aware of this when a request to straighten up the loft caused an electric locomotive to become airborne and bounce off the coffee table below. We now own probably the only copy of Linda McCartney's *Sixties* sporting a cowcatcher dent.

My neighbor Eva used to tell her daughter, 'I need you to take a nap for me.' If Stephanie protested, she'd add, 'I need you to take a nap for *me.*' Naps give everyone a chance to recharge. They're nature's timeouts. So why the change?

The kicker is, just because kids stop napping doesn't mean they don't tire. They still sometimes manage to burn out during the day. Only, they now do it at the most inopportune times. Like in the car.

Ah, the good old days, when you'd drive around for an hour hoping baby would fall asleep. When the sacred snows of diminished alpha activity finally settled on that little head, the universe underwent a chiropractic adjustment and cracked back into place.

That's changed. Junior now nods off the minute he's belted in, which usually coincides with your needing to do three errands in the next fifteen minutes. You're faced with the moral dilemma of either leaving him alone as you dash in for dry cleaning, stamps, and Band-Aids, hoping some goody won't report you to the local prosecutor looking to make a name in an election year, or *waking him.* The knell of those words. However wolverine-like an unnapped child, he's a cherub compared to one roused from a short sleep.

When kids stop napping they may also start to turn in earlier at night. You may not find this so bad as you draw the covers up to their chin and put away thoughts of chloroform. However, unless your diurnal rhythms are set to Dublin time, you may wake to find your youngster already up and about, blasting cartoons and educating herself in a variety of ways, such as how many Scooby snacks can be consumed in one sitting. You may also find yourself on the phone groggily explaining to an irate new parent why your sky-high tyke has dialed her and roused her colicky infant.

But no matter. As every parent whose kids have transitioned from nap to rap quickly points out, the teen years lie ahead—those times when it requires a winch to get them out of bed and you can't believe you ever worried about them sleeping enough. Fortunately, all that rest may result in improved academics, helping them remember Bangor isn't the capital of the Byzantine Empire. When the moment of truth comes, you'll be able to point with pride to your scholastic superstars—over in the corner of the gym, nodding off over their SATs.

Demon Dolls

The fine art of parenting, I've discovered, includes an ongoing course in needlepoint on one's nerves that cross-stitches imagined concerns onto real fears. At this point I've got a regular sampler going about Anna's ugly dolls.

If you can believe educators such as Bruno Bettelheim, horrific fairy tales, spooks, goblins and parents' high school yearbook pictures help kids surmount their fears and become more independent. I'm hoping this also applies to dolls modeled on side show freaks. When I survey Anna's hideous collection of plastic playmates, it's hard not to think the opposite is true—that they may, instead, inspire psychopathic tendencies. In which case we have a future Subway Strangler on our hands.

My worries started soon after returning with Anna from Guangzhou. Acutely aware we resemble a gingko tree as much as a Chinese couple, Marsha and I ordered an Asian doll from our adoptive support group to smooth her transition. It cost as much as a black market visa and took two months to arrive from Italy, where the closest thing to Asians apparently is reruns of *The Incredible Hulk*. With a bowl cut, troll-like features, clenched fists, and skin so hard you could hit line drives with it, it's about

as cuddly as a toilet bowl brush. Anna gnawed its feet at every opportunity. Not every doll serves as a teething ring.

Another doll, which nurses from its own bottle, has a permanently strangulated expression that recalls Luca Brasi's fate in *The Godfather.* Appropriately, the same couple who gave it to us presented Anna with a Barbie boom box, which has provided us with two years of numbing pseudo pop. I can't think of anyone we'd like to put a contract on more.

The ranks of the doll damned now also include Emily, an American Girl doll whose right eye opens half way, as if she recently got in a bar fight; a Cabbage Patch bath doll whose swollen visage recalls the baby that died in the movie *Trainspotting;* and a dark-skinned doll whose painted hair looks 'conked,' the way black people wore it before civil rights. I'm expecting a call from the N.A.A.C.P. on that one.

I always thought dolls were supposed to foster feelings of tender concern and maternalism. Anna's seem geared for Ramboesque frenzy. When I go in her room I feel I should be toting an M16. While it may bode well for ROTC involvement later on, it feels premature at this stage.

Thankfully, there's still Barbie. For all the guff about her perpetuating sexist stereotypes, she still has one thing going for her: she doesn't resemble a lineup at your local precinct. You're not afraid she'll inspire fantasies of pulling out someone's fingernails.

After the Barbie deluge last Christmas, she now nearly outnumbers her more decadent dollmates. In case of a doll Armageddon, though, Marsha and I have provided ol' Barb with reinforcements.

On a trip to Chicago last weekend my wife took Anna to the American Girl store downtown. A play, a tea, and the equivalent of a mortgage payment later they emerged with two dolls, Kit and Annie, that actually don't send you scurrying for prayer beads. Kit and Annie will be joined by Emily when she gets home from eye surgery at the doll hospital. Yes, there is such a thing. (Please don't ask me if there's an HMO for dolls, too.) This is light years away from Raggedy Ann and Andy, but, then, Emily, Kit and Annie are no ordinary dolls. They actually cause me to drop a stitch in my needlework of worry over doll-psyche connections.

I should take a cue from my neighbor three doors down. A toned softball fanatic and ski racer, Larry doesn't object to his little boy dressing up in Anna's clothes when he comes over to play. No fears about him going out as Dr. Frankenfurter of *Rocky Horror* on Halloween or putting *Little Mermaid* stickers on his training wheels.

Unfortunately, like most Dick and Jane era moms and dads, mine believed that if boys laid a cuticle on Baby Tinkles they'd grow up to join the Rockettes. I once made the mistake of cleaning my cousin's doll house when I was seven, probably because, unlike my house, everything in it matched. My folks reacted as if I'd sold classified documents to the Soviets concealed in an Easy-Bake Oven. In a twinkle I found myself deluged with subscriptions to war comics and enough make-believe ordinance to stage my *own* Cold War. Curiously, G. I. Joe was absent from the proceedings. Maybe they were afraid I'd go for a man in uniform when I grew up.

They should see me doing cross-stitch, now.

A Cacamamie Story

There was a period not too long ago when our whole life seemed to revolve around excrement. And not metaphorically, either. We were like the embodiment of that Yiddish curse about falling in the outhouse just as a platoon of Cossacks have finished a prune stew and three kegs of beer. A regular blizzard of the stuff was coming down on us.

Here's the poop:

About the time the Supreme Court was taking a dump on the electoral process, my mother started becoming incontinent, 4-year-old Anna still refused to be potty-trained, and one of our cats began using the entire house as a litter box. Had we worked double shifts packaging processed cow muck, it's doubtful our days could have been more filled with *merde*.

Let's start with Mom. You've heard about the homemaker who went ballistic when someone put a burnt match in the clean ashtray? That was my mother. For most of my life you could have mixed cocktails in her wastebaskets, they were so clean. Squirrels wiped their feet before they climbed on her patio. Dust parted for her like the Red Sea for Moses.

Then, while visiting one day, I couldn't help noticing that her living room, which from day one had reeked of Murphy's Oil Soap,

Linusitis

It's the job of parents to worry, goes the party line, and I tend to agree with that. But my parenting worries tend to be more about projected negative scenarios than physical endangerment. I'm more concerned about Anna joining the Crips one day than falling off her bike into a rose bush.

Maybe it's also a guy thing. I'll be the first to admit that men don't seem to share all of women's anxieties about kids. Maybe because we don't experience the visceral connection of pregnancy, followed by the shock of birth separation, we don't freak as much over them possibly separating head from body on a trail bike or when dunking a basketball off a stepladder. It's not that we don't care about their well-being. We just want them to test boundaries, run with the pack, as it were, and not be too hamstrung by fear.

Try and convince a woman of this, though. Since becoming a parent I've had many salutary discussions with women on the subject of child safety. Most recently, with my neighbor Rebecca, whose solicitude toward her teenage sons stops just shy of rectal exams. This woman makes Dr. Spock look like a child support delinquent. She once gave me a description of the motoring habits of a boy who drives—er, drove—her eldest to school, so minutely observed it would have done Jack Webb of *Dragnet* proud. 'Suspect emerged from house with coat undone . . . cleaned windshield without wearing gloves . . . failed to warm up car properly or observe full stop at nearby intersection . . .' It's my fervent wish St. Peter cuts us a bit more slack at the pearly gates.

Forthright soul that she is, Rebecca put my mind at ease right away on the subject. According to her I deserve tarring and feathering for child endangerment, and the only reason Anna is still alive is because she has a bevy of angels sitting at her shoulder.

My wife agrees with this assessment, especially after a recent controversy. Preparing to ride her bike through our development, an enormous cul-de-sac wherein hungry garage sale mavens are the most dire threat to life and limb, Anna inquires if she can ride down the big hill.

'Absolutely not!' says Marsha in her best DI mode.

'But Dad already let me!'

Well, yeah. I mean, she had her helmet on, and both tires were pumped up, even if one wheel wobbles a bit, and I was riding next to her, at least most of the way, because the hill in question, now that I think about it, could be used to train the US Olympic ski jumping team, and Anna was well within gold medal range when she reached the bottom. Let it be known for the record that I yelled 'Use your brake!' twice during the descent, and no Telemark landing ensued at the bottom.

Regardless, this sat about as well with Marsha as a bean and borscht burrito. Like her Jewish grandmother, who loved enumerating homicides in Miami even though she lived in Pompano Beach, my wife worries a lot. Every time Anna ventures outside, the world is ratcheted back to one million B.C., with Pteranadons swooping down to carry her off.

For some reason this panic surfaces more often in the grocery store than elsewhere. Marsha is convinced beyond the shadow of a doubt that every sexual predator and internet marketer of body parts is there when we walk in, stationed next to the cottage cheese or sequestered among the dryer sheets, waiting to pounce. With such evil lurking about, my tendency to give our daughter a long lead comes under even closer scrutiny. Letting Anna wander by herself into the next aisle could possibly lead to some of *my* parts being marketed in cyberspace.

Linusitis

'But Anna has this cloud of noise and verbiage surrounding her, kind of like Pigpen's dust cloud, which makes her easy to track—'

'You're not on *safari* with her!!!'

Sigh.

For better or worse, I'll just keep dragging that blanket around. It beats lighting candles. They've been known to singe angels' wings.

Mad Moms Club

In recent years motion pictures such as *The Joy Luck Club* and *First Wives Club* have shown us groups of women able to forge new, authentic selves from their manacled ones. Along those lines, it's time for *Mad Moms Club*, aka *Women With Stock In Spermacide*.

This film, directed by someone with poor circulation, would be about stay-at-home moms' fury and possible empowerment, and be rated R-19. That would be the insulation needed to protect the audience from onscreen rage. I'm hoping to get Owens-Corning as a sponsor.

The roles in this movie would be played by neighbors in my development. Working from home, I know where all the Mad Moms are (out in the street, usually, yelling at their kids) and can sweet talk them to work for me. Mad Moms can be dangerous. You don't want to mess with them unless you're wearing a Nomex suit.

This is one of the differences between Angry Moms—those who reasonably assert their own and their children's rights—and Mad Moms. Angry Moms have their rage under control. Cross a line with one of their brood, they fix you with a stare that makes you feel like a fly in a microwave oven and coolly remonstrate with you. If their kids are at fault, they at least wait till they're around the corner before hitting them upside the head.

Mad Moms, on the other hand, are apt to combust on the spot like a Buddhist monk war protestor no matter who's to blame. I once took issue with a neighborhood teenager about her driving. Apparently this girl took driver's ed with Richard Petty: all road signs to her are as checkered flags. My mistake was doing it in her driveway. In seconds the searchlights fired up and Mad Mom appeared, also fired up. Had I not been wearing wool, I'd have been incinerated. Needless to say, the last word wasn't mine.

That's the thing with Mad Moms: you can't ever rap their kids without risking denial. Their life revolves around their family, so everything their kids do reflects on them. Talk about living dangerously. I'd rather wade into a piranha pool bleeding than have my self-esteem subject to whether junior put road kill in someone's mailbox.

It's a shame Mad Moms are so hard on themselves. Parenting's difficult enough as it is. Outside interests or no, a lot of the time you indeed feel like you're being nibbled to death, regardless of your body fat percentage. Then you're expected to ante up for braces for those same teeth.

Granted, I'm not much into sacrifice, which I usually associate with cisterns and Mayans. If the future of mankind depended on my selflessness, our species would be on the endangered list and David Attenborough would be combing the Kalahari for us on the *Discovery* channel. I'm continually amazed that mothers are able to deal with so many demands. It seems only logical to have a life of your own to replenish all that giving.

My mother-in-law sometimes tells Marsha, I love you more than life itself. Great, I say; *you* tell Tank the garageman she can't pay her tab. When I hear such things, I can't help wondering how many mothers would be better off loving their own lives a bit more.

So get out of the house, Mad Moms, and not just to run Eric to T-ball. Get a makeover. Get a horse. Get a NASCAR membership. Let your kids squabble over leftover Spaghetti O's once in a while. It's better than throwing yourself in a volcano of rage.

Meantime, cattle calls for *Mad Moms Club* start next week. Note to casting director: keep a heat shield with you at all times.

Playdata

Christmas break has just concluded, and I feel like chilling out. Make that being cryogenically frozen for awhile. Of the fourteen days Anna was home from school, eight involved play dates, of which she and I, the dad who works from home, hosted seven. Any more, and we'd have to flag a spaceship to bring us back to earth.

This routine is new for me. Though I often played in other kids' yards, I hardly ever went in their houses. Mom claimed I was allergic to a great many things, starting with air, so other abodes were dicey. Hardly anyone came to my house, either, for the same reason: they got tired of her following them around with a can of Lysol, as though they were mold.

So the past two weeks have been sort of a playover boot camp for me, a combination of feeling like Gomer Pyle and Joe Frazier after the Thrilla in Manila. That parents similarly conscripted may go the full fifteen without being quite so woozy, the following observations may help.

Just A Spoonful Of Sugar Makes The Seismograph Go Round

For some reason snack manufacturers aren't content unless their products contain the entire sugar cane harvest of south Florida. Dry snacks like pretzels are your best bet, in place of a bungee cord, to keep the kiddies at treetop height. Unfortunately, the selection of beverages is more limited, water being the only one among a parade of juice boxes and fizzy drinks that couldn't be labeled *POTENTIAL CHERNOBYL II*. If you plan on having a great many playovers, a retractable roof—financed, perhaps, by neighborhood extortion—might be a good investment.

Warning: Predators Afoot

Do not, under any circumstances, schedule a play date if you suspect you're even one T-cell short, unless you want a crash course in Jung—specifically, that business about *animus* and *anima*. Kids scent weakness on par with a hyena, and will see your diminished energy as the perfect opportunity to try bobsledding down the stairway on a couch. And even if they don't feel especially mercenary, you won't be up for the usual demands of playing 'dead babies' (no, I don't know which standup comic Anna got this from) or disengaging someone from a ceiling fan.

The same goes for inviting kids over who have recently tusseled with scarlet fever or some other malady that will spread through your household like grease from the garage floor.

Two's Alright, Three's Not Allowed

It's been said that one child is a family, two or more a conspiracy. For the same reason, unless you've engaged a S.W.A.T. team for its duration, a playover should never include more than one guest—it will always be two against one, and all against you. Even the Three Musketeers couldn't cope with that.

The Bulkhead Drill

Normally done a split second before that little depth charge drops on your front step, it involves a screaming dive for the doorhandle of every room you wish to remain off limits; your bedroom, for instance. Little girls, especially, *love* to dress up, and your wife may not appreciate her lingerie being employed in this manner. Forestalling access to the K-Y as potential Barbie hair gel ain't such a bad idea, either.

See You In Sing-Sing

Face it, there are only two types of children who come to your house to play: (1) yahoos with raccoon eyes who fasten clothespins to your cat's tail; (2) kids who build a replica of the Hubbell telescope out of a Slinky. It's your job to screen out as many of the first as possible, perhaps by offering them a nice snack from the last batch of Halloween candy—*yours*, from 1970—that will have them running all the way home from your door to theirs, never to return.

Little Hands, Big Mess

The Big Bang theory, I'm certain, originated in the aftermath of a playdate. Unless you want to spend a billion or so years rounding up minute particles of matter such as Ello pieces, it's a good idea to enlist the aid of the perpetrators before the gathering disperses. This will teach accountability and perhaps plant the seeds of a Gandhiesque attitude toward the material world which will eliminate your co-signing Visa apps in future.

Hello, You Must Be Going

In our experience two hours is about right for a play date. Longer than that is living on the edge of the volcano, especially if you lack a basement to contain the magma. The exception is when, for some reason found in the deepest recesses of your psyche, you allow a playover to morph into a *sleepover.* In which case disregard all of the above and bed down with your dog in the foyer. You won't have to queue for the bathroom in the morning.

First They Drive You, Then They Drive You

I'm noticing a lot more things in my street these days, such as kids in cars with their parents riding shotgun, learning to drive. Last week these kids were riding bicycles and leaving them in the driveway to be run over. Now they're running over their bikes themselves.

It's always nice when children assume responsibility.

Kids have a funny way of growing up. They go along for awhile, not seeming to change at all, then, one day, you notice something, and it's like a bolt unsticking. Like their coat hangers suddenly being large enough only for doll clothes. That they're now putting conditioner instead of spaghetti sauce in their hair, and have a KEEP OUT OR UR DEAD sign on their bedroom door. That their back-to-school shopping list, which used to contain items such as glue sticks, crayons, and notebook paper, now reads, 'bong, Bose, cooler.' (They saved the glue sticks over the years to sniff between classes.) Or that you have to tap your 401(k) to pay your car insurance bill, especially after sonny mistook the back of the garage for the brake pedal.

We won't be faced with the driving issue for several more years, which should give us plenty of time to get therapy to deal

Boo-Hoo Box

I was transplanting a hosta in our back yard when the sound reached me, a shrill keening spiraling from our daughter Anna's room. Shortly afterward my wife appeared above me at the landing window, shoulders agitating like a cocktail shaker, her face distorted with grief.

This has happened before. It generally means one of three things:

(1) We are hormonal. You must live in the kindling box the next three days.
(2) QVC just sold out of the bracelet I wanted.
(3) My credit card interest for last month equals the GDP of Mozambique.

As it turned out, none of these applied. 'She was so cute,' Marsha wailed as tears coursed down her cheeks. Aha. There could be but one other explanation. She'd been into the Boo-Hoo Box.

The Boo-Hoo Box is our version of the proverbial child's keepsake chest, a contraction of 'Boo-hoo, our baby's growing up' box. It contains all of Anna's stuff that we can't bear to part with plus anything we'd get into a fistfight over trying to sell in a garage sale and the consignment store would give us less than three cents for, anyway. Things like her first little dump truck, her Anna Banana tee shirt from the eponymous store on Plantation Key, her first pair of soccer cleats.

The Boo-Hoo Box began as a nondescript cardboard container no bigger than a sub-woofer that Anna routinely crushed trying to get at things in her closet. It's since morphed into a plastic tote the size of an Ohio River barge. We're confident it will eventually hold her first car, which she has informed us will be a Volkswagen Beetle. It has special meaning for us because Anna is an only child and will probably remain so unless one of her friends lodges in the chimney during a playover. So whatever goes into the tote stands not merely for 'little Anna' but for early childhood, period, that precious time of projectile vomiting and reeking Diaper Genies—I mean, of pre-cognitive innocence. It has mythic significance.

For Anna, it's just old stuff. Partly from having grandparents who overspend on her so severely she's still opening birthday presents four months later on Christmas morning, she views it more pragmatically, the way an assembly line worker might regard yesterday's product. What we see as being sprinkled with fairy dust, like her first set of tub toys, she sees exactly as they are: plastic boats stippled with mold that we couldn't scrub off. As they say, nothing is more distant than the recent past, and that evidently applies even if you're seven years old.

Something tells me that may change, though. As the merry-go-round of childhood picks up speed between school and soccer and swimming and dance and social lepidopterism, Anna may feel more inclined to jump off now and then to revisit the days when an entire afternoon could be spent taping the Tupperware together or eating a bowl of Rice Krispies one at a time. A day may come, even, when Barbie numero uno will migrate to summer camp or dorm, carefully obscured in the foot of a sleeping bag, to be less carefully extracted at a suitable point in the proceedings ('Dudes! Let's all bob for Barbie in the beer!')

For the moment, all the boo-hoos are ours, and not just for Anna. I've noticed the cataract of keepsakes is slowing somewhat. This may partly reflect an increase in toy size. It's a lot harder to fit 'my first ten-speed' into a box than Mr. Potatohead. But as her playthings become more sophisticated and adultlike and the daily routine more intense, Marsha and I may, without knowing it, be becoming equally casual about archiving Anna's past. In other words, we may be losing some innocence ourselves, as parents. Which is why we'll always have a Boo-Hoo Box—to remind us some things are worth keeping to miss.

Even if it means crating a VW now and then.

Squirts and Dirt

Childhood, that precious time of sugar and spice and everything nice, of snips and snails and puppy dog tails.

Try again. That stench o'rama filled with acres of boogers. That goat-reeking aftermath of days spent at the park gathering algae from the pond and dog poop on sneakers.

As a parent now on the shop vac end of such grodyness, I find it easy to disparage it. And for that reason, perhaps, I sometimes long for those days when I could eat a tomato out of the garbage can with gusto, and a smudge on a pair of white shorts didn't drive me to paroxysms of self-hatred. When, in eighth grade, I could go an entire school year without washing my gym clothes and feel a sense of accomplishment about it as I presented them to my mother. (I think she burned them in the back yard. Perhaps not coincidentally, the community where we were living at the time, Cleveland Heights, became the first in Ohio to ban open fires. A number of people downwind were probably asphyxiated.)

No question about it: if cleanliness is next to godliness, most kids are professed atheists. Dirt has a decidedly different molecular structure for them than it does for adults. It doesn't inspire panic or disgust in them. If a grown person finds a hair in his chili while eating out, he'll send it back, probably at a speed that Pedro Martinez rarely achieves with his 'heater.' Whereas your average toddler will cheerfully chow down a saltine that has lain for months in a cat hair-clogged corner of the broom closet. To him, it's just a nicer-tasting Brillo pad.

As kids grow and start to differentiate the palatable from the amoebic in their world, a funny thing happens in their attitude toward dirt: nothing. This is because of the age-old family dynamic, *cogito ergo up yours*. Translation: if adults hate it, kids can use it to their advantage to piss us off. We should never underestimate the value of dirt to kids. It's very special to them, a form of revenge against the million and one rules, regs, restrictions, and restraints they face every day. It's chaos they can control to some extent. And unlike, say, a bedroom that looks like the aftermath of a hurricane, it's portable, a protective bubble they can transport with them on either their person or their clothes.

In either form, dirt is especially useful to the social outcast. One of the most unpopular kids I knew in school elevated body odor to a high art form, ignoring soap, mouthwash, and deodorant. Inevitably seated next to a window, he'd lift the sash, then his arms, and maybe cut the cheese for good measure, letting the breeze circulate his stockyard reek round the classroom. Mustard gas was never more effective: within seconds nearly everyone would be passed out or comatose at their desks. Despite mediocre grades, there was never any question of him 'passing'; I'm surprised he didn't graduate from college at twelve. This person is now a major corporate player, perhaps employing the same methods in the conference room.

Thus far, Anna has shown little inclination to use obnoxious effluvia as an existential pawn. (What would be the point, when baths offer a nightly opportunity to create even more chaos? If we kept a walrus in the tub, it's doubtful that more water would wind up outside it. We're thinking about removing the molding and installing scuppers instead.)

Nevertheless, there is the matter of hair. Anna remains unconvinced that it's part of her body and thus eligible for hygiene. Without us chivvying at her, she would cheerfully let it fuse together, Rasta-like, with dirt. Marsha, in fact, contends that Anna's first words were 'no wash hair.' Despite utilizing an array of shampoos and conditioners that would keep Cousin Itt of the Addams Family fluffy, we've so far been unable to make hair washing more attractive than taking a laxative.

Hopefully, this is just another of those little sticking points that, lubed by the passage of time, frees just before graduate school. Anna's cousin Erin, who wore her hair long, had a similar attitude toward hair care, and resolved it herself. After returning from a cruise with so much salt in it that it was feared the extra weight would congeal neck vertebrae, she had it bobbed, which made washing and drying it easier. We suggested this to Anna, and got told that 'good Chinese girls don't cut their hair.' That's in China, we say—interestingly enough, a country where water is at a premium, yet they still manage to keep their hair clean.

With any luck, this appeal to ancestral pride will do the trick. It's a bit early to start wearing wigs.

NOT A TRANSVESTITE: ESPOUSAL ISSUES

Crazy by Halves

Depending on the circumstances, just about anybody you encounter in daily life can drive you crazy. It's how they do it that determines if you wear a polo shirt or a straitjacket to the office on casual Friday. As they say, that which doesn't kill me makes me stronger, though not equally neurotic.

There's a world of difference, for example, between the person in the next cube who sits sniffing all day, and the one who pesters you on deadline about whether you want Swiss or Provolone on your sub. One inspires thoughts of grenades lobbed at close range, the other at least makes sure your belly doesn't derail your train of thought.

Similarly, the banshees, Marsha and Anna, sometimes make me want to hop a freight, but ultimately drive me nuts in ways that are beneficial. They know that, left to my own designs, I'd probably wind up alone somewhere in the Outback, counting links in the dingo fence, my brain and body mush. So they devise ways to keep me on the narrow, just shy of strait.

Continuing the down under metaphor, Marsha has an ongoing project of turning our treadmill into a miniature Ayers Rock. It sits buried beneath a mountain of unread books, unseasonal outerwear and undressered underwear; potentially, an entire Nautilus gym: just clearing it gives me a complete aerobic work-out. Following suit, Anna treats laundry hampers as a sacred aboriginal spring not to be defiled, leaving clothes wherever they happen to be shed. Wading through this stuff, which gathers around my ankles like lead weights, keeps both my physique and attitude toned. It's hard to be overly concerned about world order with such chaos underfoot. Call it the *tao* of *hao*sekeeping.

Over the years my charges have also kept watch over my immune system—by making sure I have plenty of sustenance verging on lab-appropriate.

Unlike other culinary kahunas, who tend to belong to the Clean Fridge Club, Marsha loves to cook but not to eat leftovers. She also believes that even if a stomach-stapled midget is the sole dinner guest, she should prepare enough servings to satisfy the population of Trenton. So our fridge winds up a food museum, with yours truly the curator. Like the ancient king Mithridates, who immunized himself to poison by taking a little each day, I consume enough penicillin to cure myself of anything except the inability to pitch victuals before they walk away under their own steam. If any more green fuzz passed my lips, I'd turn into a Chia Pet.

Anna compounds this by rejecting any food not prepared to specs syllogistic as calculus. I stand over the cutting board unsnarling possible peanut butter sandwich scenarios, such as: 'She likes more jam than I do, which soaks through potato bread faster than wheat, so I'd better use more pb to sop it up in case she brings it home; also, to make sure she gets enough to eat, because if she *does* eat it she'll leave the crust anyway . . .'

Such tortuousness benefits my powers of reasoning, which helps with Anna's inquiries. After that, why carrots are better than candy and whether or not God has both breasts and a penis seems like a piece of cake. Frosting on the side.

But if there's one way in which Marsha and Anna have contraried me to health, it's by keeping the local power company in business. For some reason—unaligned meridians, perhaps—'off' switches remain off-limits to them. They fall asleep, go outside or to work and school leaving the house lit up like a casino, TVs going, CD Roms playing. This has brightened my outlook no end, and not just pineal-ly: it's encouraged me to be debit-minded.

Like most people without a Swiss bank account, we've taken our share of hits financially the past few years. But as our portfolio attests, solvency comes in paradoxical ways:

—value of my investments: down 50%

—value of Marsha's: down 37%

—value of largest single stock in my account: down 63%

—approximate savings from turning off lights and appliances over same period: $32,000,000

As *Monty Python's* Eric Idle used to sing, always look on the bright side of life. Even if it's half in shadow.

Sickness in Style

Do men enjoy being sick? In a piece from *1–800–Am-I-Nuts?*, called 'In Sickness and In Health,' humorist Margo Kaufman contends that 'unlike women, men basically enjoy ill health,' and quotes several males as proof. '"When I get sick, I feel great," confesses Glen, 38, a lawyer . . . "Getting sick is one of the little tests men have for women," opines screenwriter Rob, 32.'

To hear these guys talk, you'd think they were lining up to be injected with mad cow disease.

We need to define terms more closely here. For starters, though it's been used before as ordinance in the war between the sexes, this isn't a gender issue. Men don't enjoy being sick. No one does. We obviously enjoy making others sick, with things like poison gas and Olestra, but I have yet to meet someone outside the S & M coterie who truly enjoys pain. Illness is a drag that limits mobility. Think of Larry Flynt, housebound for years. With Mrs. Flynt. Scary.

What men do enjoy is being devious and manipulative—like women—and minor aches and pains are a great way of being both. Being a bit sick is like being slightly wealthy: you get to enjoy some of the perks without being kidnapped for ransom. It's a win-win situation. Call off work with the sniffles and it's your ballgame, as long as your boss doesn't see you at one. Go in, you get plaudits for being super-conscientious and, like as not, sent home early to channel surf.

The real question is not whether men take advantage of women's nurturing by exploiting finger aches but whether men and women use sickness for different reasons—for attention, plane tickets south, or whatever. In my experience, they do. Marsha and I are perfect examples.

Contrary to Ms. Kaufman's thesis, I like oceans of space around me when ill. The worse I feel, the more I want to be on an atoll in Micronesia. Sickness appeases the solipsist in me. It hearkens back to childhood, when my parents, anticipating managed care, encouraged me to suffer in silence until gangrene was about to set in. One trip in an ambulance, they reasoned, was more cost-effective than multiple visits to a GP.

Just as well. Fate has contrived a curious way of keeping codependence out of my cough syrup. When I'm sick, not to mention broke and downhearted, my wife inevitably is away on business. As a butterfly's wings have been found to riffle the atmosphere a thousand miles away, every sneeze of mine wafts Marsha farther afield. It would be a bit much to summon her from a conference in Scottsdale to brew me echinacea tea.

On the other hand, my better half envisions herself as the Martha Graham of illness, and choreographs her surroundings accordingly. She turns the living room couch into a domestic version of an Antarctic substation, with everything from nail polish to computer solitaire an arm's length away. And whatever isn't within reach can, of course, be procured through her faithful gun-bearer. It's no longer 'Molo, bring whiskey-soda,' as in Hemingway, but

Advil, *Vogue,* afghan. Memsahib's demands keep me beating the bush.

A double standard? Maybe. But I can't honestly say it reflects a power struggle. In time it may rank up there with whose bagel gets toasted first. For now, keeping well is the best medicine for both of us.

Morning Gory

A few minutes ago I saw a commercial in which a Nordic beauty threw open her window to the morning sun, the curtains billowing behind her as a fresh breeze winnowed her blond mane and she closed her eyes with a smile of perfect bliss.

How depraved. Why anyone would break into an aria just because morning has broken is beyond me, and always has been. When it comes to greeting the day with enthusiasm, Dracula's got it all over me. Supposedly I was the first infant ticketed for a U-turn at birth, and kept pestering the maternity nurses for sunglasses. I can't ever recall leaping out of bed, except one time when I thought the room was on fire.

Marsha, of course, is different. While the rooster is still spray-gelling his comb she's flitting about trilling Sondheim melodies and brimming with brio. 'Best time of the day!' she twitters as I pull the covers over my head and groan. She can't understand why anyone would act as though battery acid rather than daylight were seeping through the blinds. 'Sometimes I wake up grumpy, and sometimes I let him sleep,' she adds, wafting downstairs to climb K2. I hate her.

Mercy, indeed, is something I never expect in a country nurtured on Poor Richard's 'early to bed, early to rise.' My education in early morning morality began in grade school. At a parent-teacher conference it was pointed out that simply because my last name started with 'Y' didn't mean my grades should also come last. My teacher suggested that perhaps I had trouble learning because my head was inside my desk all the time. My mother confirmed this, observing that I frequently came home with crayons up my nose. What could be done?

Being British, Mom found it irksome that the sun should set on any portion of the Empire, especially beneath a desk lid. In best lance-sergeant fashion, she turned every morning thereafter into a reenactment of imperialism, including a clarion call to arms—nicely served by her voice, which acquires the brassiness of a fishwife's when raised—and a simulated cavalry charge to my bedroom, the uncarpeted stairs resounding like a thousand hoofbeats in my brain. I was thirteen before I realized I wasn't starring in a remake of *Gunga Din*. Such measures failed to improve my morale but did earn my mother a citation from the National Guard.

In later years the method was refined. It was found that a breakfast of chocolate milk, chocolate cookies and chocolate cake could at least persuade me to catalepsy before 9 AM. This behooved me during high school when the registrar, in league with Argentinian torturers, kept scheduling me for gym first thing in the day. Teamed with a lot of jocks who'd stayed up as late as 8:30 the night before, I was whipped into the best shape of my life running back to the locker room to barf. I became the most feared offensive (and I do mean offensive) threat in class simply because no one would lay a hand on me; I'd have coated them. Eventually my peers got sick of wiping off the ball and I was given first period study hall my senior year, which I passed peacefully in a corner of the cafeteria under a pea coat. Had the cleaning staff not alerted me, in fact, I'd have missed graduation.

Thankfully, those days are long gone. As a mature adult I've discovered the one thing needed to cope with circadian difficulties: self-employment. It's a win-win situation. Not only does setting my own schedule eliminate a lot of morning malaise, if I finish work a bit later as a result, the neighbors are impressed. They assume anyone who eats dinner while watching David Letterman must be a workaholic. And if the banshees have to tiptoe around me first thing in the day—well, I'll make it up to them at Christmas. It beats replacing battered alarm clocks.

For Better or Worse, Indelibly

People sometimes talk about long-married couples being as comfortable together as a pair of old shoes. That's nice, but in my experience marriage is a different sort of attire: a suit that you both wear and wear and wear, and it gets thin in the seat and frayed at the collar and cuffs, and some stains wash out and others don't. But you continue to wear it because the cut still basically suits you, no matter how often your partner draws attention to the grease marks.

Sometimes those stains arrive in the strangest ways.

Our friend Bob's father lives in a neighborhood with 37 bars, 35 of which he usually samples after work. That's about one bar for every year of his marriage. (I'm not suggesting, of course, that there's any correlation.) This is apt to make him a bit testy at dinner.

One evening he flipped a supposedly underdone hamburger up at the kitchen ceiling, where it stuck for a while before plummeting into the jello. Ever since, the minute he starts grousing at mealtime, his wife smiles a knowing little smile and slowly inclines her head, as if toward rapture. Bob's father could now be president of a temperance society and that grease stain, long since sponged away, would still be on his ceiling metaphorically.

Not a Transvestite: Espousal Issues

As years go by in a relationship, indiscretions take on the character of original sin. No haj or act of contrition seems to erase them. Even if your partner isn't especially vindictive, the right circumstances can trigger an almost Pavlovian response. Whenever I question Marsha's taste in movies, she immediately counters by broaching Fred Schepisi's *The Chant of Jimmie Blacksmith.* Unaware of what a downer flick it was, I once took her to see this aboriginal ax murder revenge parable at a local college film society. The print was so bad it looked like hordes of locusts were flying across it. Never mind that we've since seen scads of fine movies at my recommendation. I could be on the Cannes jury every year and my cinematic taste would still be impugned by *The Chant of Jimmie Blacksmith.*

Don't get me wrong. I'm not suggesting that partners generally, let alone my own sugar-booger, spin themselves into a Sufic trance trying to get the drop on each other. Merely that certain unfortunate incidents of an extreme nature acquire archetypal significance over time. They become like relationship rosetta stones, referenced again and again no matter how remote the original circumstances.

Sometimes, even time itself functions this way. Marsha and I have vastly different attitudes toward it. In my hands it becomes like Salvador Dali's soft watches, pliant and gooey, whereas she treats it like an air traffic controller, believing that being a nanosecond late automatically qualifies you for the stocks. Personally, I fail to see why you should get to a kid's birthday party on time when, most likely, the parents are still in a back bedroom wrapping Blo-Pens. Unfortunately, because of one exceptional instance of tardiness, my opinions on punctuality count for nought.

Full disclosure: it wasn't so long ago when, if I showed up on time for something, the nearest governing body would call a press conference. I was late so often for school that, contrary to my transcripts, I actually held myself back two grades. It helped keep my weight down, because there was never any food left when I got to parties and I usually wound up walking everywhere after missing my ride. But women hated it. Those who stuck around long enough, anyway, to arrive at ball games in the bottom half of the first. It never occurred to me that the only time coming late was appreciated was back at her place or mine.

With one exception, I was never *that* late. But that once I was 2½ hours late for a picnic with Marsha and her family. I was arguing with my first wife over the Visa bill after she'd charged a Lamborghini, and the argument became a chess match. By the time I arrived even the ants were into the Bromo Seltzer.

Never mind that one of my in-laws is usually so behind with meal prep we eat before going over for dinner, or that I've since cleaned up my time act to where I no longer even have ushers for acquaintances. When it comes to letting go of this issue, Marsha is into Crazy Glue. Not even a pilgrimage to Big Ben, I suspect, would put time on my side.

The one redeeming thing about these grease spots is, they're shiny. Paradoxically, this makes them an incentive to stay married. Because if you're together long enough, eventually there will be so many of them that you'll think you're wearing sharkskin. That beats a pair of old shoes any day.

Once Smitten, Twice Shy

As the novelist Thomas Wolfe once wrote with redundant flair, you can't go home again. Put another way:

You're sitting at a red light dreaming of cheeseburgers when you notice a former main squeeze in the car next to you. Do you:

(1) roll down the window and invite her (him) to dine at Wendy's?
(2) smile ruefully into the distance while contemplating the curious juxtapositions of fate?
(3) burn rubber so severely when the light changes that a cop pulls you over for ozone depletion?

If you answered (1), hope that there's a motel behind the restaurant. Baby, you've got it bad. (2) wins you the DVD version of *Casablanca*, (3) a front-row seat for my Sam Kinison routine.

Not that I don't have some good memories from previous relationships, if I bang my head against the door jamb hard enough to dislodge them. But I can't imagine anything more difficult than returning to an old flame. I'd rather return to seventh grade history class, sitting next to the kid with chronic b.o. With relationships, I get the feeling hindsight isn't 20/20, it's Ted Williams's vision the year he hit .400. You look back and think, what was I *on?* No matter what the circumstances of parting, there's embarrassment mixed with the bittersweet, and it extends beyond matters of taste and maturity.

After all, presuming you weren't just another notch on their knickers, the other party has known you long enough to be wise to you—to know who wiped out your speeding tickets, or how you garnered those backstage passes to meet Lenny Kravitz. Which, presumably, they've informed everybody else about this side of Alpha Centauri after you broke up. When the blinders come off, so do the gloves.

I'm always amazed when I read of someone, usually a celeb, saying of his former spouse, 'We're still good friends.' Right. Like the only reason they split was because he was shooting on location so much or she needed more space to pursue astrophysics. If they're still friends it's because she got enough alimony to cover their kid's shrink bills and he lives in a walled compound with a housekeeper schooled in Jeet Kune Do.

But at least they're living separately. What about estranged couples who, after all those ugly scenes and dirty little secrets, not only start seeing each other again, but remarry? After which, with the benefit of perspective gained from time apart, they proceed to beat each other's brains out all over. (Look at Liz Taylor and Richard Burton: twice married, twice divorced. If they'd really wanted to please each other, she'd have bought a distillery and he'd have procured a diamond mine.)

Talk about gluttons for punishment. It's hard enough even to be casual around former companions, let alone start cleaning their bathtub ring again.

Marsha and I once had the bright idea, after we started dating, to invite the guy she had broken up with three months earlier to go boating. Now you know why neither of us was ever tabbed for Mensa. Happily, nobody was found floating facedown in the shallows the next day, but the static in that cockpit would easily have plugged the blackout of 8.16.03. So perhaps the ultimate discouragement for going home, however briefly, to that little igloo of an old attachment is the most basic: you may die. Especially if you're attached to someone new. That's healthy. It helps you get on with life. It also helps you avoid exercises in futility like school reunions, where, guaranteed, one of the following will happen:

—If you're female, the ex-detention hall mainstay who once left his fingernails in your waistband will stagger up to you and boozily exclaim, 'Hey, it's old Legs-In-The-Air Delaney!'

—If you're male, the lynx you dated who now models machine shop calendars will, with equally inebriated enthusiasm, regale your companion with the tale of how she had her first multiple orgasm aboard your chopper.

Either way, the armrest may be down between you on the way home.

Handbag Hell

Men's pursehandling skills are so poor we can't even wear a fanny pack properly. Zipper bags, so indispensable to dropping a month's salary at Sea World, traditionally are worn either facing rear, so that we can be deprived of our valuables discreetly, or slung low in front, as if we're auditioning for Chippendales. You'd think we could at least remember how the West was won and wear it on our hip.

How sad. There are times when pockets just ain't adequate. Especially if you're packing a few extra pounds in thighs and tush. Stuff wallet, change, keys into pants, you're risking a rash if not a wedgy. Seated, you feel like you're perched on a coconut. And you don't exactly endear yourself to cashiers when, after prying coins from your pockets for half an hour, you also hand over a fistful of lint.

Then there's the sheer melodrama of purse ownership that we're missing. Boffing the Other (Wo)man over the head with it. Sitting on it when you visit a grungy relative. The seasonal ritual of changing handbags, which Marsha looks forward to more than sweet corn.

We need help. Couturiers, traditionally so adept at garnering the female buck, need to step into the fold, the billfold, and appeal to our vanity. At least one has accepted the challenge. Designer Louis Vuitton recently retailed a shagreen purse for $21000. With a handbag like that around, who needs a set of gold golf clubs? You could stow it in your Ferrari with room to spare. Enough for a carton of truffles.

Baby's in Black
(Not Me, Thank You)

In a makeover worthy of a MacArthur genius grant, my wife, a fashion maven, has transformed me from a perennial walkon candidate for *Oliver* to someone who can walk through a store without being tailed by security guards.

For awhile I resisted it. So what if the seat of my pants was threadbare, or my collar sported more mends than fabric? When you're raised to wear stuff till it resembles cheesecloth, that's only the beginning of its usefulness.

In time, though, the allure of not being an attire retread grew, along with my wardrobe. Dressing respectably had its perks. I not only stopped getting noticed for the wrong reasons, but got attention when I needed it. After catching the eye of even chain drugstore personnel, a feat on the order of cloning Michael Jordan, I said *adiós* for good to disco era duds, hello to Oxford cloth and khakis.

On one sartorial point, however, Marsha and I still chafe: the role of black in your wardrobe. In her eyes, black is the foundation of style, a cornerstone of couture without which the entire fashion industry would crumble into meaningless detritus

Women's Shoes: A Scream

My wife unveiled a new pair of shoes the other day. Ordinarily, this would be like saying, 'Germs recently were detected in a boys' locker room.' As a sultan with hundreds of wives could go an entire year without visiting the same one twice, ditto Marsha with her footwear.

This pair was different, though—more like ordinance. 'These are my man killer shoes,' she said, booting an imaginary placekick as she went out the door to work. 'Kill' in this instance I suspect doesn't mean leaving staggering with laughter around the copy machine, but receiving last rites. They looked like they could take out anybody, regardless of species or gender. Slingbacks. Heels like clips for a 9mm pistol. Shark gill slits on the side. Toe somewhere between pointed and square, like a snapping turtle snout. Carnivorous shoes. They could eat Lennox Lewis, if they didn't consume their wearer first.

Women's shoes are one of life's enduring mysteries. For some reason I thought that when you pawned the silverware for a new pair of pumps they shouldn't leave you limping like a Civil War reenactee. What a concept. Comfort is so alien to women's shoes that it surfaces around them only humorously ('Lesbians:

women in comfortable shoes'—Robin Williams, *Good Morning, Vietnam*) or obversely, as when Marsha and I are walking in a strange city and she gets a look suggesting an attack of cramps, starts clumping along as though wearing snowshoes, then hails a cab to take us back to our hotel, two blocks away.

It should be obvious by now that the real threat to women's lib is not mossback conservatives or ingrained semantic tendencies but the designers of women's fashion, especially shoes. Forget barefoot and pregnant; anyone who keeps half the species broke and crippled can teach a bondage seminar anyday. Let's look at how women's footwear enslaves, using the aforementioned 'mankillers' as a paradigm.

More Off The Back, Please

As with all women's fashion, the principle 'less is more' applies: less material in the shoes, more money in the designer and manufacturer's pocket. This is especially obvious in the back of the shoe, which often is reduced to a single strap or eliminated altogether, a far cry from the hightop boots of 100 years ago which let women safely wade through horse dung and male imperiousness. The paring-down of women's shoebacks has resulted in two outright abominations over the years:

(1) Clogs. Undoubtedly the creation of an ex-Peace Corps volunteer yearning for the sound of African beaters driving lions through the bush. One woman wearing these gunboats on asphalt tile could singlehandedly create the soundtrack for an earthquake film.

(2) Mules, which nearly ended our friend Val's marriage before it began. Emerging from a favorite watering hole one night with her fiancé Larry, and feeling no pain except in her feet, she kicked off one of her Borax busters in the general direction of Polaris. A couple of ticks later Larry was crumpled on the parking lot, clutching his head, which now bore a dent the size of the Arizona meteorite crater. Someone called the cops, and the two lovebirds found themselves on their way to EMS in the back of a squad car at 1 AM. Their wedding pictures feature Larry with hair combed over his forehead like Peter Lorre to hide the damage.

Feeling The Crunch: Pointed Toes

Let me get this straight: women recoil in horror and righteous indignation from pictures of Chinese foot binding, then cram their toes into footwear that somehow has escaped the attention of Amnesty International's Campaign Against Torture. And we wonder why the equal rights amendment failed. After owning a pair of Beatle boots (briefly), I can personally attest that one evening in this type of shoe leaves your feet in a condition to pick locks. Any and all pointy shoes should be labeled Hammer Toes In Training for the uninitiated.

Spare The Leather, Ma'am

It was cool when the Sex Pistols wore ventilated clothing during the punk era. But unless you're hankering for a tetanus shot, wearing shoes that contain more air than leather makes as much sense as fighting in a paper tank. I mean, shoes are supposed to protect your feet, right? Isn't that why we wear them?

Steal This Heel—Please!

Right. We now come to the apex of either fashion befuddlement or genius in women's shoes: high heels. Foot doctors and those who believe only performance artists should suffer for beauty take the former view, because high heels tend to result in the following:

—tendons, ligaments and arches like an Amtrak pileup;

—holes in any surface walked on, including granite;

—herniation of the lower back—especially his, if you wear them while making out;

—a tendency to want to mate with Kareem Abdul-Jabbar.

On the other hand you have the following data, from Linda O'Keefe's *Shoes:* 'According to *Harper's Index,* the average protrusion of a woman's buttocks when she wears high heels is 25 percent . . . an erect ankle and extended leg is the biological sign of sexual availability in several animal species. . . . spike heels . . . force the leg into what anthropologists call a "courtship strut."'

There, you have it: healthy feet vs bootylicious. You get the feeling that companies could curb sexual harassment by encouraging women to wear flats. Though it might be more effective simply to make them aware of the maiming potential of their footwear. High heels, not to mention pointed toes, air holes and straps, could provide pretty convenient handholds for beating back the importunate. If a randomly launched mule can nearly ice someone, imagine what pumps wielded with intent could accomplish.

In fact, some strategically-utilized women's shoes might have saved America a bundle in addressing recent national security issues. Instead of invading Afghanistan and Iraq, our government should have forced inmates at Guantanamo Bay to wear stiletto heels till they confessed the whereabouts of Osama bin Laden and his cohorts. They'd have been in custody within hours. Instead of spending a fortune to beef up scanners, hire additional guards and train flight attendants in *krav maga*, airlines should have begun issuing a pair of Marsha's mankillers to all female and cross-dressing male passengers as they boarded.

Richard Reid would have soon lost the urge to martyrdom.

AUTOMOBILES AND OTHER BETA BLOCKERS

Carmudgeon

It has come to my attention that the Amish are consulting to the automobile industry. This may seem odd, because hardly any of them drive, let alone own cars. But they do have this saying about 'getting too soon old and too late smart,' and carmakers seem stuck on designing product as if we're all senile.

With temperatures rising on America's streets toward the melting point of lead, it's nice that certain vehicular innovations have become standard. Things like power door locks and fuel injection give us precious additional seconds to make our getaway from the crazed SUV commando we failed to yield to, while 'lights on' bells spare us getting stranded in neighborhoods where 'lights out' is the rule for anyone stationary.

Unfortunately, cars also are being marketed with features that take the place of common sense and standard motor skills. Sensors that switch your headlights on. Sensors that engage traction control. Sensors that tell you to change the oil and fasten your seatbelt. (What we really need is sensors that tell you when you have spinach in your teeth.) These gratuitous features drive up the cost of driving, making cars more expensive to own and fix. You used to establish a trust fund for your kid's college education. Now you do it to replace a timing belt.

They also create a safety issue. With cars practically driving themselves, motorists become prey to distractions, doing stuff behind the wheel they used to do in the privacy of their bathroom. At one time, picking your nose was the closest you got to performing mobile hygiene. Now we do everything short of a colonic (but watch out if they ever put a Water-Pik holder on your console). Likewise with dressing and undressing. Within recent memory you were unclothed in a vehicle only when mooning someone or getting it on. Now we practically hit the road with a valet. One newspaper columnist has confessed in print to putting on panty hose while driving. Tell me she didn't have cruise control.

Maybe driving a Cadillac, with monthly payments approaching those of a beach shack, entitles you to more bells and whistles than a steam locomotive. But a hydraulic trunk? Close it part way and it closes itself the rest. Obviously, this car is being marketed to demographics that no longer have the strength to pull their zipper up. You have to wonder if they should be driving at all. If they can't close their trunk lid, maybe they can't turn the wheel fast enough to avoid your dachshund. (If GM really wanted to be cutting-edge, they'd design a trunk with a hydraulic lift that would load your groceries as you chase your three-year-old across the parking lot.)

It's possible that urban sprawl, with its longer commutes, is encouraging superfluous auto technology. People spend more time driving to work now than watching the tube. So why not design something really useful, like bucket seats that convert to composting toilets? That would not only take a lot of steam out of innerbelt traffic but eliminate, in no uncertain terms, a trip to the garden center, saving fuel.

At a certain point a car that's more self-monitoring than a space capsule is just another back seat driver. With cars, as with kids, there's a fine line between smart and smartass. A smart car is one that can fit into a parking space meant for a skateboard or take you to Tunisia and back on a tank of fuel. A smartass car tells me I'm low on gas when my wallet's empty, making me feel like Jerry Van Dyke in the '60's sitcom *My Mother The Car*. Only, instead of ragging on me to drink my milk, *it's* the one that's thirsty.

But there's hope: even with all these innovations, cars haven't become as space age as engineers once envisioned. You can't yet program your Honda to avoid the Lotto store or the sale at Nordstrom. Maybe even auto makers are leery of cars becoming so smart that they take over completely. If that ever happened, at least one of us would be in line for the auto-da-fe.

Out of State, Out of Mind

What is it about road maps that's so off-putting? I get the feeling just about everybody, at one time or another, would rather consult a cardiologist than a map. And would need to: forty-three wrong turns en route to an appointment can easily induce arrhythmia.

The last I checked, maps are not a controlled substance. Possession of one will not land you a mandatory 10 years without parole. The profession of cartography is ancient and venerable, predating even Kitty Carlyle Hart. So why does the great American love affair with the automobile turn frigid when it comes to pulling over and looking at a grid?

For one thing, they're usually hell to use. I just bought a Rand-McNally road atlas; in a quarter-century of driving it's the first map I've opened without hearing a polka in my head. All those folds, which never realign themselves correctly, and try isolating the section you need on short notice. Driving's nerve-wracking enough without an impromptu origami course.

Ego may also be a factor. Brainwashed by jouncing vehicles in TV ads, the voyageur in us finds release by blindly plunging into unfamiliar terrain. Poised behind the pommel of our

SUV, we fancy ourselves a frontier scout, navigating thickets of traffic with the ease of Kit Carson. Unfortunately, we don't count on a line of concrete barriers or an overturned 7UP truck diverting us into unfamiliar gulches ten minutes before show-time. Without a bent twig to guide us, it's intermission before we know it.

There's another variable, too, I think, harder to nail down but just as important, that explains our aversion to maps or even asking directions: the nomadic impulse, an inability to break stride, involving, especially, dads. I've yet to meet a father who could be persuaded to pull over except by a police siren or a blowout. The development of the interstate has only fueled this obsession with movement.

Though he never mentioned it, I'm convinced my own fa-ther was born on an express train. He obviously believed that, once he put foot to pedal, stopping for any reason would likewise cause the earth to stop rotating. As he liked to take long trips, ac-companying him proved an enlarging experience in at least two respects: I now have the bladder capacity of Lake Baikal, and if my ballhandling skills matched my peripheral vision I'd lead the NBA in assists every year. At 60 mph it helps to take in as much terrain as possible at one glance.

Even under pressure, people seem more inclined to con-sult their horoscope than pause to reconnoiter. Just ask the dri-vers who deliver pizza in my development. If these guys flew a plane the way they drive, they could skywrite in Hindi. With only seven streets down here, they think it's a no-brainer to find one. Unfortunately, all of them are dead ends, so they end up career-ing around the neighborhood like horses in a thunderstorm. Those hot bags must contain a microwave.

Admittedly, maps do get out of date, leading to conversations such as:

'When did they divert the St. Lawrence Seaway through here?'

'I dunno.'

'How old is that map?'

'Uh, Gerry Ford was president when it was published.'

'@#$&*!'

Credibility can also be an issue if you stop for directions. My rule is never, even when late for an audience with the Pope, inquire at a service station, especially self-service. These people hate cars. Really. They will go out of the way to send *you* out of the way, if you can get their attention. Usually you end up playing verbal ping-pong with the clerk through a window while a guy ahead of you buys Marlboros and Gummi Bears. After ten minutes of volleying, with your kids yowling in hunger and your wife clicking her TMJ so hard it feels like an earthquake, you finally get an answer: the Indonesian restaurant you're looking for is now buried beneath the gas pumps. Which leaves yet another question:

How many Gummi Bears equal a serving of *nasi goreng*?

These Wheels Were Made for Walkin'

My friend Myles, formerly a bounty hunter, has his sights on something else now: buying a house. But first he needs some better wheels.

Myles used to be the baddest guy around, riding in a pickup with a shotgun in the back window. When he glared at you it was like looking into an open hearth furnace. He was the only guy I knew for whom pit bulls held the door when he came calling. Mess with him, he would cheerfully refund your life expectancy.

That's all behind him now. Myles gave up his gun a while back along with his attitude. Unfortunately, in the 'hood you either pack heat or risk feeling it. That's why he wants to move.

Myles rents the upstairs of a house on Cleveland's near east side. His neighborhood is the opposite of mine. Where I live you see cautionary road signs showing a man on horseback. In Myles's area that would mean mounted police. On my street the neighbors keep up with the Joneses; Myles's have a jones. My neighbors, all of whom have central air conditioning, keep their doors and windows shut. Myles's have an open door policy: leave a door open, they'll clean your place out, then offer to sell your stuff back to you. Disrespect is lobbed back and forth like a live grenade. Somehow Myles holds aloof. Without reliable wheels, he's stuck.

Myles's swaybacked Monte Carlo is 20 years old. It's broken his bank a number of times. Its bald tires pick up so many nails we've christened it Voodoo Chile. It needs jump-starting so often it might as well be an electric car. It's so temperamental it actually encourages DUI: before driving it you toast with saki like a kamikaze pilot.

Cars like that remind me of cats (I speak as a former AMC Hornet owner.) They toy with you. You think you own them, but in reality just feed them. Dollars. They hang around, more interesting than useful, extending a pawlike piston into every nook and cranny of your life, especially your wallet. You find yourself dating body builders because they may have to help push. A tow truck becomes your second car. You tend to work near bus lines so you won't be stranded. Myles has found that just getting to and from your stop can be like playing a lethal board game. With a couple of drug points, a crack whore, and several gangsta canines to circumvent en route to work, his negotiation skills now surpass Richard Holbrook's.

I'm less confident. Myles gets off work late, so I usually visit him at night, when he's not watching *Star Trek* reruns. Even so, in that neighborhood my pickup resembles Starship Enterprise—every light's on, the brighter the better. (I must be the only motorist with a halogen glove compartment light.) The last time I drove down his street someone yelled at me that Mardi Gras was over. But at least the truck prevents misunderstandings: my Saturn tends to attract an armada of the pharmacologically challenged to his house. Never underestimate the impact of sporty taillights.

These Wheels were Made for Walkin'

Now that Myles has a better job and is saving some money, he dreams of buying a duplex elsewhere. Of being the landlord for a change, sitting on his porch without a bullet-proof vest on. But it's tough scoping out real estate from public transportation. So every cent not spent bungeeing Voodoo goes toward a new car. Sometimes he gets despondent over making up so much ground. I tell him at least one vehicle in the neighborhood is worse.

An elderly wino lives in an abandoned sedan in an adjacent lot. He's been there over a year. Cops ignore him; neighbors avoid him because he smells. Stray dogs figure that, because he relieves himself against Myles's house like they do, he must be one of them, so they don't sweat him either. Some nights my friend can hear him singing. It reminds him where wheels can and can't take you.

Have Suction,
Will Unravel

I just got sucked into buying a $1700 vacuum cleaner. No, that's not an extra zero. And I wasn't trying to jumpstart the American economy singlehandedly; it just sort of happened. In my living room. I'm still trying to figure it out.

Perhaps because door-to-door salesmen are a vanishing breed, I've forgotten how to deal with them. I've become so used to blowing off nameless, faceless telemarketers and direct mailers that when an actual live merchandiser shows up, it's like a black rhino has appeared. They have this aura that leaves you agape, wondering how many gun barrels they've stared down recently, and before you know it both feet are in the door. This is a far cry from incidents like the following, which were common at my parents' house:

Having somehow negotiated the pillboxes, mines and SCRAM welcome mat that graced their front porch, a boy about seven, carrying a handle bag, is hammering with a landlord's insistency. This does not bode well for him. Anyone who compelled my folks to answer the door they treated like something crawling out of a cargo hold. The storm door has almost shattered with the force of kiddie's blows when my dad yanks it open. Though only

5'4" tall, he grew to the size of Ursula in *The Little Mermaid* when affronted.

'Stop that banging!' he shouted. 'Whaddaya want?!'

'You don't want no candy?' the kid croaked.

'No!' *Ker-pow!*

(It could have been worse. A member of the Hare Krishna sect once departed *wearing* his copy of the Bhagavad-Gita. For all I know, there may be a Fuller brushman or two enriching the soil at the old homestead.)

I now look to this incident as all epigoni regard the glorious deeds of their ancestors, with a mixture of wonder, longing, and shame. The taste of ashes is in my mouth as I crouch on the sand under a threadbare blanket, feeling the wind whistle through my wallet.

I suppose the fact that our last three vacuums sucked eggs should console me: a can vac that wouldn't inhale a dandelion pod, another that kept flipping on its back like a sprayed roach, and an upright which required a course in safecracking to change the bag. We get flyers for this one all the time. The company prez stares at you as if calculating how many more sales he'll need before selling to the highest bidder in Bulgaria.

Unlike those, this machine deserves a niche at the Smithsonian. It's streamlined, quiet, with wands for suctioning drapes and shampooing carpets. Hooked up to a syringe, it would probably have the power to do liposuction. It's so versatile that Pigpen from *Peanuts* could visit every day and we'd still be presentable. Is it worth $1700? Let's put it this way: it's the last cleaning apparatus of any kind we'll need, Handi Wipes included.

I have to admit, the salesman knew his stuff, changing attachments so fast my head spun like a beater bar. He showed us how the clutch worked. That's right, clutch. Poured enough table salt on our carpet to purify a Sumo wrestling match, and sucked it up. And every so often he'd drop a hint, while fingering a reward program in his pocket, about how close he was to earning a vacation in Acapulco. At the conclusion of his spiel, when he saw me waffling, he brandished this sheet with evangelical fervor, as if trying to replicate an ocean breeze. I expected him to drop to one knee and break into a rendition of *My Mammy.*

At this critical point in the proceedings I looked to my life's companion for much-needed dissent. When the mood suits her Marsha can prepare a dish of Rocky Mountain oysters from just about any merchant. Given a choice between solvency and selling the place settings, however, she'll eat off paper. This time she did her level best to impersonate a bobbing-head doll. The salesman practically capered about the living room. He was so excited I feared we'd have to break out the shampooing hose prematurely.

Mercifully, we got credit for a trade-in. Between this, the clutch and the price tag, we practically need a registration and stickers to operate our new appliance. We also received a video instructing us how to use the various attachments (just as well: we won't be renting any movies for a while). Now all we need is a can of Simoniz to keep the aluminum hood shiny. With enough light, you can see yourself scratching your head in it.

Heavy Petting

My friend Myles, also a seasoned hardware store vet, was keeping me abreast of the trade. So, what's the biggest seller these days, dude? I asked. Glue traps? Window caulk?

'3/8 inch chain, to Rottweiler and pit bull owners,' he said.

Somehow, I don't think this is how we get back to a bull-ish America.

Though there may be some cute ones out there other than in the *Carl* books, put horns on a Rottweiler and it could star in a rodeo. As for pit bulls—Myles has seen young men walking them past the store with bricks in their mouth to strengthen their jaws. Presumably, not so they can carry home a bag of eyebolts. We're a long way here from Old Yeller.

Unfortunately, there seems to be a growing trend in Ohio, even outside Myles's neighborhood, toward owning dangerous pets, if you can call them that. Would you 'pet' a mongoose? They qualify as pets only by being kept in captivity. Which means one other thing: even if you put up electric fences with Joan Rivers's face posted on them as a deterrent, these creatures will try to *get out.* They're wild. And it's been happening. In recent memory:

—A python surfacing in a Shaker Heights toilet. Talk about a sure cure for constipation.

—A black mamba—the world's deadliest snake—at large in Akron. Try getting vaccine for that at Kaiser.

—A full-grown lion killed by authorities while roaming free in southern Ohio. And you thought skunks in the trash were a problem.

To my knowledge, no Noah's ark grounded in the Buckeye State, and none of these creatures was liberated by animal rights crusaders. They all escaped from private owners. Was OSU's game that boring this year, that someone needed a python to curl up next to them on third-and-two? And it seems unlikely, even with people eating at home more since 9/11, that culinary considerations were involved. I haven't noticed a market for javalena burgers here. Yet.

You expect to read about a boa constrictor gobbling someone's chihuahua in Hollywood, or a gator drowning a 71-year-old man in Florida, because you expect fruitcakes with more money than sense to own snakes as big around as ATV tires and build condos in alligator alley. But in the corn-fed midwest, the beer gut of American common sense?

Unless you have a death wish, there's no point in owning a creature that sees you as dinner. Personally, I have no illusions about nature: if it's moving toward me I'm in reverse. Karma does not apply to wild animals. So what if you cried as a kid when

Bambi's mother died? Accidentally spook a grizzly while photographing the great outdoors, no previous eco-mindedness or promise of prints to the Sierra Club will buy time for a getaway. *You* will receive prints—on your sternum. So why put your life at risk? Buy a budgie and dye your hair blue instead.

I mean, there *are* such things as zoos, funded with your tax dollars, where you can observe all manner of teeth and talons up close without worrying about beating a cheetah back to your car if it doesn't like your cologne. Not to mention slaughtering a steer for its keep.

Is it being consumed by possessions (at the risk of them consuming you) that impels us to buy dangerous animals? Or simply the illusion of mastery over nature? We forget that animals learned the ropes of survival before we did. They don't think it's bad manners to bite your nose off instead of rub it; they're just doing what comes naturally. Frankly, if it were my nature to run down live prey, and I saw gramps next door taking his time to the mailbox, I wouldn't let a little chain link bother me.

As for impressing the neighborhood, there are less potentially litigious ways of doing it than raising Komodo dragons. Though, admittedly, few discourage block parties as well.

Et Tu, Tattoo

From time to time you get these subtle hints that the world is leaving you in its wake. Such as that more and more of your business associates are younger than you. That the people now graduating from college weren't even a zygote when you donned mortarboard. Or that everyone except you seems to be getting a piercing or a tattoo.

Correct me if I'm wrong, but it used to be that if you got a tattoo, or got an earring and were male, you were either a sailor, gay, or of so liberal a mindset you thought psychotropic drugs should be dispensed with the McElhenny's in restaurants. Now even the Young Republicans across the street who equate the Statler Brothers with Slayer have them.

I find this mind-boggling. Needles and skin mix about as well as onions and sorbet. The twain should never meet unless it's for medical reasons.

To me, the only sane reason for a tattoo is to remind you where you left your car keys; a piercing, to give you a convenient place to hang them when not in use. Though I recall reading about one stud who had a bonking couple stitched between his shoulder blades. When he flexed his back muscles, they gyrated accordingly. Turning yourself into a human sandwich board does seem rather resourceful.

I can understand the impulse to utilize every available medium for art. My father, a superb draftsman, drew on everything from tracing paper to tree fungi. But he didn't go around stabbing himself with his calligraphy pens.

A problem with using yourself as the canvas—apparently easy to forget in the flush of getting *JUNIE* stitched across your midriff—is that the medium may become more permanent than the message. You may feel somewhat conflicted displaying such sentiment after Junie has pawned your Roger Clemens autographed baseball and migrated elsewhere. In which case, you now have two choices:

(1) You can opt to live with this misplaced reminder of transitory attachment for the rest of your days. Every time you stand in front of the bathroom mirror in the buff you will have visions of your ex- buffing her new boyfriend's, um, kickstand, and of your memento fetching untold thousands at auction. You may also have trouble convincing any future romantic partner that *JUNIE* is the Hindu avatar you once named your pet gecko after.

(2) You can have the offending artwork burned off with a laser, a process considerably more painful and expensive than the original tattooing, which may leave the affected area looking like it's been chewed by rats.

It's been said that body art and jewelry, especially among young people, represent an inversion of energy: unable to muster the drive and desire to move out of Mom and Dad's basement and pursue a degree in entomology, they start impaling themselves instead of bugs. Presumably the pain involved assuages any guilt. You'd think they could accomplish the same thing more economically by removing their toenails, one by one, with a pair of pliers.

Not that the abundantly tattooed self-absorbed are necessarily all slackers. Consider David Beckham (aka The Human Inkwell), the English soccer player competing for Real Madrid. Once the standard for midfielders, he now finds himself compared in the Spanish press to Forrest Gump for his enthusiastic but ineffectual play. Unlike Forrest, who was tattooed only in the but-tocks, Beckham has ten. Carting around all that dye may be wearing him out. It's a wonder he doesn't get booked more often for diving.

The thought of Anna turning even one part of her anatomy into a pincushion, of having it possibly turn septic, slays us. (Oh, for the good old days of *inner* ear infections.) We might as well be talking about a bone through her nose. Fortunately, in our household such issues are settled reasonably and democratically: if Anna shows up on our doorstep before the age of 18 stuck with anything more permanent than a mosquito bite, she'll be conscripted to work at Dy-Dee Wash. At least there, any needlesticks will be accidental—from safety pins mistakenly left in the diapers.

Cease and De-list

As the holidays draw near it's easy to get bogged down in lists—wish lists, guest lists, grocery lists, to-do lists—their entries scrolling out of sight over the horizon like railroad sleepers. And despite all this regimentation you may find yourself forgetting things and becoming disorganized. Listless, even.

Relax. This is the perfect opportunity to stop scripting everything and simply go with the flow, letting your memory prioritize what really needs to be done. Chances are you'll still be spending Christmas eve in Toys 'R' Us whether or not 'must have' items are written down.

Time management gurus will scoff at this. These people, of course, think life is a meaningless void if you're not grafted to a legal pad or Visor 24 hours a day, making lists and excising them. They frequently tell you how much pleasure they take in crossing things out. It makes you wonder if they have an orgasm when they hit their Delete button. You can visualize them in a guard house somewhere in Sakhalin, scanning a list of transgressors— 'Ah, corporal Nivaeskin was found distilling vodka from dirty socks again'—then smilingly drawing a heavy line through one of them.

Cease and De-list

List-making, supposedly, lets you exercise greater control over your life. But when it becomes equivalent to creating anti-matter, it's time for a bit of randomness.

Sometimes it helps to consider the entire context of a word before treating it as a mantra. The other meanings of 'list' include:

—a place where knights engage in horseback demo derbies;

—a boat leaning to one side, often just prior to giving its passengers an up-close look at marine life;

—spelled with a 'z,' a Hungarian virtuoso who inspired large numbers of women in the audience to pass out.

Violence, instability, and rampant horniness, all possibly leading to cessation of consciousness. Sounds pretty chaotic. Hardly the sort of association that reflects well on an organizing principle.

But to be fair, let's consider some concrete reasons why lists may not be all they're stacked up to be.

They *could* be turning your short-term memory to mush. It's that 'use it or lose it' thing. And just as using a calculator may dilute your math skills, note pads and Palm Pilots may water down your focus with additional anxiety, especially when they disappear down a storm sewer. Better to rely on mnemonics that spin the tumblers of your brain, such as 'arf/barf'—buy heartworm pills and baby wipes.

Nor do they necessarily save you time. Henry David Thoreau comes to mind. When asked why he didn't ride the newfangled steam train to Fitchburg, he replied that he could make it there under his *own* steam by nightfall, whereas the train might not arrive till tomorrow. The same with lists. You sit there notating stuff you already know you have to do, trying to anticipate contingencies, while time ticks away. When you finally hit the trail—littered with convoluted phone menus, red tape and orange barrels—you're already behind, and about to get further off the pace when you're pulled over for converting a 25 mph zone to metric, or taking a shortcut through Safari Land. Better to just get at it.

There's also the potential clutter of lists themselves. If you throw away the list at day's end regardless of how many things you've accomplished, no problem. But if you're like me, you tend to hoard lists rather than transferring undone items to new ones, as if that would make time stand still so you could catch up. Especially early in the week when I'm fresh, I bite off more than I can chew (a typical Monday might include installing a water garden in my yard, getting my tires rotated, and reading *The Rise and Fall of the Third Reich*—before lunch), so the spillover ripples through the rest of it. As I use Post-Its, by Friday my computer monitor looks like my dad's face after he cut himself to bits shaving and stuck toilet paper all over it.

Dad, in fact, was a compulsive list maker. It made his studio as much fun to clean as a Rococo drawing room. It may have been against his religion to have more than three things on a piece of paper (usually miniscule—I think it was his secret ambition to paint vast panoramas on postage stamps). He also liked to duplicate lists. So whenever anyone sneezed in his vicinity, it was like shaking a snow globe. When one of us had a cold he'd disappear for days at a time. We had to keep sled dogs handy even in the summer to find him.

Frankly, I'm inclined to agree with Einstein that God doesn't play dice, at least on streetcorners. So if you forget to pick up Cheetos on the way home because you didn't write it down, don't despair. *You* won't be on someone's EKG list.

Corporate DIY

A man in England recently made medical news of the sort that makes me nervous. Even more so than the one who plans to impregnate himself with his own sperm after having a sex change. Never accuse the British of not making- do.

Seventy-two-year-old John Phillipson underwent bypass surgery while wide awake, receiving only an epidural injection instead of general anesthesia. The *UK Mail* reports that he laughed and joked with surgeons during the procedure, and later that day was able to sit up in bed and read. He was discharged two days later and is doing well.

Now, I have nothing against Mr. Phillipson, and hope he lives to endure many more servings of Vegemite. What concerns me is that he may be setting a dangerous precedent. He may unwittingly be contributing to an unhealthy trend in society. Call it corporate DIY.

In recent years businesses have been putting more and more of the burden of customer service on customers. Utilities are eliminating bill paying stations. Banks have ATMs, supermarkets automated checkouts, and the full service gas station is going the way of VHS. You can't even talk with a service representative on the

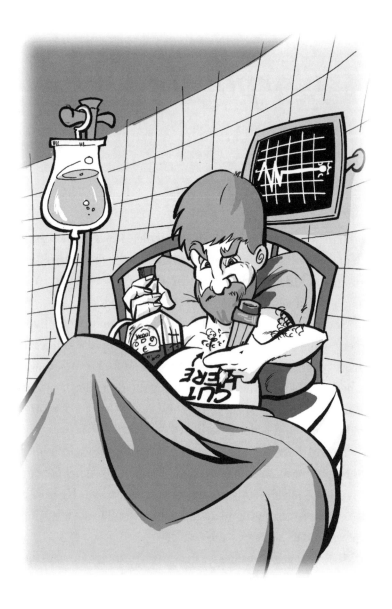

phone without first negotiating a menu that would baffle Garry Kasparov.

Get my drift? With John Phillipson undergoing heart surgery with scarcely more fuss than having a root canal, can the day be far off when we're asked to operate on ourselves? I can see it now: we'll be given an anatomy chart with the offending area circled, supplemented with an old recording of 'Dem Bones,' a tray of surgical instruments and sutures, a bottle of either Biofreeze or, if you're on an HMO, Old Grandad, and a room (with a checkout time), and left to our fate.

Think I'm overreacting? Riddle me this, Batman: whatever happened to 'the customer's always right?' Gone, dead, kaput, because there's no one around now to listen to you. Somewhere along the way a bean counter figured out that if we were always right, then maybe we didn't need that much help to begin with. So companies eliminated experienced personnel and replaced them with gadgets and employees who receive ten minutes' training and can't answer you beyond 'Aisle 11 B.'

And what have we, the consumer who keeps these businesses alive, received in return for diminished overhead and increased profit?

Savings? That may have been true once, when DIY was tailored for the customer. People built their own garage or pulled their own brakes because it was more cost effective. They saved on materials and didn't have to hire anyone. But I don't see my bank offering me free checking for using their ATM, or the supermarket discounting my food for cashiering it myself. And the only self-serve gas station I know of where you can consistently save is run by people who also own a pizza parlor (even small businesses are getting into the act), and it's positively third world.

The pumps aren't digital, so a fill-up takes forever; there are no squeegees, trash bins, roofs over the pumps, or card swipe. It's one step up from stopping at a tin shed in Mali to take on fuel from Mr. Kourou's 55 gallon drum. The only benefit to this place is price, and I have a feeling that's because the owners cut the product with tomato sauce. I'm afraid to patronize it too often in case my fuel filter gets jammed with anchovies.

Of course, an uglier shopping experience that doesn't give you cash back can still be made to sound like a gift, by resorting to that all-American rationale, speed. No more need to stand in line, just push a few buttons and out you go.

Uh-uh. This line of reasoning fails to take into account two little variables which can actually make self-service slower than usual.

The first is that some of us have brains wired so far to the right that sharpening a pencil equates to high tech, and just the thought of translating instructions on a screen into motor activity on a keypad sends us into paroxysms of confusion. So that after we've accidentally jammed the self-serve register by putting coins in the bill slot, called for help, and migrated shamefaced to the conventional checkout, we already could have been home counting the change we've lost.

Second, I think think-tankers have seriously undervalued the perception of value received. I used to really enjoy having a guy wipe my windshield, check under the hood, and kick my tires while he filled 'er up. So if I've got to do all that myself, and get gasoline stink on my hands to boot, I'm damned well going to avail myself of everything there. I'm going to use the restroom, buy a *Tradin' Times*, maybe string a hammock between the pumps and catch some rays. What used to be a filling station is now a trailer park. No way am I getting out of there faster.

So from a customer standpoint there's really only one benefit to corporate DIY: convenience. If you get a hankering for Pop-
Tarts at 1 AM and don't feel like standing in line for the one cashier
working at that hour in your local chain supermart, you can scan
them yourself and slouch off to Bethlehem with your sugar fix.

Just don't make it a habit. You may have to implant your
own insulin pump one day.

Food Free

Next to the cartoons and crayoned stick figures tacked to our refrigerator door you'll see a couple of magnetic messages that Marsha has placed there: a shocking pink-lettered STOP sign and a metaphysical-sounding question, WHAT NUMBER AM I?

The first is a variation of the cheesecake shot women display to remind them not to reach for the rest of the Ben and Jerry's Chubby Hubby. The second is more cryptic. A Zen koan it's not, though I've meditated on similar thoughts while waiting for a tune-up. Like the STOP sign, it's part of a weight loss program that Marsha belongs to that has lightened her checking account considerably. On a scale of 1 to 10, it asks, with 1 being stomach-pumped and 10 being Monty Python's Mr. Creosote, how full am I? Being honest with yourself in this way supposedly will lessen your chances of getting on Lane Bryant's mailing list or being mistaken for an outbuilding.

Believe me, it's effective. I know because every time I look at that sign I crack up and forget about eating. I've dropped so much weight the past few months that my neighbor's whippet tries to bury me when he sees me. The humor derives from being reminded of a bumper sticker I once saw reading WHERE AM

I? WHERE'S MY CAR?, which, being affixed to a vehicle, ranks with the best of Dan Quayle.

Marsha thinks I'm being flip. 'Can't you see the difference in this body?!' she cries, crushing my head into her midriff. Of course I can, even with two black eyes. Slimming is a noble objective, certain to give any relationship a lift, even if it causes your face to sag. So convinced am I of this, in fact, that I'm planning my own weight control program.

It's called FOOD FREE, a spinoff of fat free, so much in vogue these days with the weight conscious, and will be based on diversionary tactics similar to the humor mentioned above. Properly adhered to, they'll have you looking like *your* child's stick figures in no time. A sample:

Food Fights

Those tender family moments out of Norman Rockwell, with everyone sitting around calmly and rationally discussing the day's events, look great on Thanksgiving cards, but in real life only enlarge the waistline. Better the dinner bell should signal the beginning of another round. Think how much more quickly your plate empties when its contents are airborne! You'll actually expend rather than consume calories ducking a whirling cutlet or a comet of mashed potatoes. An occasional china Frisbee shattering against the wall also helps rid your house of tacky heirlooms.

Gross-Outs

My mom and dad honeymooned by car in Quebec. Short on funds, they made a point of eating at rural bistros downwind of livestock pens. In no time at all they looked like Giacometti sculptures! Negative ambience is important when trying to shed pounds. At home, try keeping your pet's cage or litter box in the kitchen—you'll be too nauseated to prepare food, let alone eat it. The ultimate, if you're lucky enough, is to have on hand an elderly relative who passes gas along with the salt or a teenager who tells booger jokes. You'll never belong to the clean plate club again.

Table TV

The ultimate in food free measures, or table rasa. Table TV combines the urges to throw and throw up in a highly flexible format. You can watch television either before, during, or after you eat, with the same result: rising adrenaline coupled with a rising gorge. The food you choose will be the food you lose. I recommend keeping plenty of large cloth napkins handy to wipe off the screen.

The key is to always watch the news. Local, CNN, it doesn't matter. One week's serving of sniper killings and government pork will have you so thin you'll be afraid of slipping down a storm drain. Caution: practicing this method longer may result in your attacking the TV station with frozen entrees.

Nutrition Attrition

A recent conversation with a nutritionist yielded the following dietary conundrum. According to her I was eating too much starch, equal to a cup of processed sugar a day, and thus could hire myself out to Atlas Cinemas as a walking snack bar video. I was eating too much starch on the recommendation of another nutritionist, to curb my craving for sweets.

If this proves one thing, it's that moderation in all things is best, especially when following advice about nutrition.

Sometimes I think more contradictory blarney has been written about food than any other area of human experience, including whether or not Eleanor Roosevelt was gay. It's the one thing we need daily to survive, so anyone who knows a lipid from a bioflavenoid feels obliged to put a spin on it. The current state of nutritional mores in America resembles the Russian economy after Communism collapsed, except that instead of Arkady's henchmen we have to worry about stuffing ourselves with empty caloric speculation.

Accordingly, we need to remind ourselves of a few basics about nutrition. (These apply only in America. The rest of the world either has trouble finding food to begin with and have to eat whatever they can, or more affordable health care, and can eat whatever they damn well please. You don't think the French would be stubbing out Gitanes in their bearnaise if they had private pay, do you?)

FIBER—Helps cleanse the system of toxins, such as the urge to contribute money voluntarily to pay down the national debt. Recommendation: consume a minimum of three nutritional guidebooks a week (printed in soy-based ink, preferably). They're at least as tasty as rice cakes and, being paper, may eventually serve a dual purpose.

FAT—Also doubly useful, storing energy and cushioning vital organs in punchups after football games. Found in nuts, legumes, dairy products, red meat, and the crania of headbangers. Should be overindulged only by latter-day Elvis lookalikes and people who work in buildings with elevators.

SUGAR—A form of carbohydrates, needed for energy and staying awake to watch Conan O'Brien. Too much sugar can be life-endangering. I once pulled a chocolate bar out of my pocket while shopping at a natural foods store, where carob—the nearest thing to edible charcoal—was the drug of choice. Judging from the response of those around me, this was roughly analogous to a Muslim chowing down a pork chop while circumambulating the *k'aaba*. I escaped with all appendages intact, but only after prostrating myself before a block of tofu.

SALT—Nowhere has the prevailing wisdom about nutrition pivoted more than with sodium. At one time it was on every table, in every recipe, even for fruit cocktail. Athletes used to be fed enough of it to make Lot's wife envious. As 70% of our body is water, we in effect were turning ourselves into miniature Dead Seas. Now you practically have to go out in a field with livestock to get it. Adding salt to anything you might as well, in the eyes of dieticians, be sprinkling tobacco over it. If you have a real craving for salt, the best advice is to bear in mind that gardeners use it to kill slugs. (They also use beer, but who wants their taste for that ruined?)

PROTEIN—Absolutely essential to health, a true cornerstone of the nutritional Ghiza pyramid. Consumed in proper quantities, it builds strong teeth, bones, nails, and hair to die for. Too much of it, however, leaches calcium from your system and could result in your looking like a dromedary camel in old age. To determine if you're eating the right amount, book a package tour to Egypt at the first opportunity.

FOOD COMBINING—Ideally, this should extend beyond tequila and limes. Combining foods correctly, such as complementary proteins (beans and rice), enhances digestion and brings out their optimum flavor and nutritive value. Combining foods incorrectly, such as protein with sugar (peanuts with lemonade) will give you the grumblies and possibly lead to being ejected from the cineplex. The Hay diet (not the one for horses) maintains that protein and carbs are best eaten separately. So start peeling your sushi.

YOUR IDEAL WEIGHT—A touchy subject, technically not within the scope of food parsing per se, but crucial to its portioning. Dependent to a degree on body type. If you're ectomorphic—tending toward leanness—you'll be able to eat more of your kid's birthday cake than if you're endomorphic—built like a rutabaga. Also affected by self-esteem. If you're skinny but overly weight-conscious, you'll be more apt to eat things that plump you up and make you feel worse. Whereas if you're sweet on size 16, you're not only heavy but happy. Even dieticians won't contest that.

Make Mine Mistakes

It's time to do some hard thinking about boners.

Most self-help books I've seen recommend you make peace with your mistakes. Tell you to accept and learn from them and move on, letting them generate sympathy for your fellow mortals as you stare at them from the back of a squad car. Treat them as a one-night stand, basically.

But as we all know, one-nighters can reappear in the form of a paternity suit. Put another way:

You're standing in a supermarket, trying to decide whether to serve your kids a green salad for dinner which they'll treat like sewage or the mac and cheese they like that will have them on a gurney when they're eighteen. The sound of water interrupts your train of thought—and it ain't the produce mister.

Next to you is an individual attired in the jacket of a team that cost you big bucks in the office pool last Sunday. A stalactite of snot hangs from his nose. He's slurping his nails like a soup bone as he squints at the endive. And you—

You've had a rough day. The Dow did a Brodie, your grade schooler wants a piercing in her eyelid, and your landscaper weedwhacked a certain plant you were cultivating behind the garage. The milk of human kindness has temporarily curdled in you. So you put it in gear and head for the macaroni one aisle over, thinking you'll just stew the box.

And there they are again. And again. At the dairy, the frozen, even in front of the Depend display where hardly anyone goes, wetly gnawing themselves. You don't realize how distracting they are till at the checkout you find you've bought rawhide chews for your goldfish.

Mistakes resemble this person. They send ripples through your life. Remember trading phone numbers with that devil worshiper in a sports bar? For three months afterward you got a collect call from Satan every time the Rams won. Or the great deal you got on a 'southern' LTD? The owner unfortunately neglected to mention that meant south of the Rio Grande, where it had one oil change in nine years.

Technology has made it worse. It used to be that if you bartered a few bad chickens you had only the neighboring village to contend with. Now you can wipe out half of Idaho. And thars guns in them thar hills.

This can make self-acceptance difficult. Remember Nick Leeson? Here's a guy who got in over his head and took an entire company down with him. A 200-year-old securities firm. You think he's standing in front of a mirror every morning murmuring, Never mind, you're basically good at heart? Of course not. He's saying, 'Go big two!'

The sanest method I've seen of dealing with fallibility is mentioned in Norman O. Brown's Freudian view of history, *Life Against Death*. (This book can justify an entire liberal arts education. You might be a toll collector the rest of your life, but at least you can say, I made it through *Life Against Death*.) Brown contends that since our brains are a road map of channeled development, the way we truly individuate ourselves is through error.

Now, there's potential. Don't merely accept your misfires, celebrate them. Allow them to express your essence. Laid off because of incompetence? Cut a demo titled 'Say It Loud, I'm Sacked and I'm Proud.' Michael Moore will be in touch shortly. Cut a power line while installing irrigation in your lawn? Take it to the limit: build a hydroelectric dam and sell power to your neighbors. Or be the first on your block to send a letter like this to the IRS:

'My sincere apologies for failing to pay my taxes since the first Gulf War. I think you'll agree that this exceptional oversight calls for an equal degree of clemency. I know we can be pals.'

If this sounds too much like denial, you could always take the Eastern approach and think of life as one big mistake. All your successes would be errors. And snafus would be business as usual.

As Charlie Chan might have said, sounds like a case of mistaken identity.

THE FRESH PRINCE OF BACK HAIR: INTIMATIONS OF MORTALITY

Whole Latte Love

An era has ended in our household: Marsha and I no longer order coffee by mail. The Starbucks Encore card goes into the junk drawer with the pizza coupons and leftover Laffy Taffy from Anna's trick or treat stash.

For awhile, being jetset java-ites was fun. Every two or three months a FedEx box arrived from Seattle bearing bricks of beans with exotic names. Guatemala Antigua. Arabian Mocha Sanani. Ethiopia Sidamo. Just placing an order was like being a world traveler. Friends who dined with us asked if they got frequent flier miles. Not having to go out for specialty coffees, especially as our favorite cafes tended to become hair salons after six months, was sweet.

In time, with Starbucks opening on every streetcorner, mail ordering became unnecessary. But the real issue was too much caffeine. With shipments of joe arriving like clockwork, we found ourselves drinking more of it and, not coincidentally, spending all our time in orbit. Aggravations such as Anna turning Mommy's bathroom into an abattoir with red nail polish put us out there faster than a Saturn V rocket. At the height of our coffee snobbery our door knocker should have been engraved with 'we have liftoff' instead of our name.

The obvious solution was to drink decaf. But, as with all drugs of choice, the meat was the motion. Those hearty brews made even decaf Sumatra seem like malted milk. We missed the buzz. We'd become caffeine junkies.

As the A. C. Greene of coffee consumption, I never envisioned such a problem. A. C. (Alternatives to Coition, presumably) Greene, a former NBA forward, travels the country counseling young people to hold onto their virginity longer than T-bills. Maybe to balance Wilt Chamberlain's exploits (though that might take an entire monastery), he supposedly relinquished his own at the age of 28.

That particular standard eluded me, but I was past thirty, believe it or not, before I tasted coffee. In America, that's like not owning a telephone and a car at the same time. For most of my life the smell alone revolted me. Forget the crisp morning air campfire stuff; for me it meant the hearty aroma of burning cadavers: charred bacon and links, with a chaser of instant coffee. An otherwise passable cook, my mother never made it past the suttee experience at breakfast. I'd watch her and my dad dissolve what looked like rust in their cup and guzzle it, and I'd dissolve, too. The mere sight of Maxwell House's Cora or Folger's Mrs. Olsen on TV turned me green as an unripe 'mountain grown' bean. For years I had to walk to school in the street to avoid being clipped like a hedge.

Much later, with memories of immolated food repressed, I found a little caffeine in the morning lifted the spirits. Under its influence I even joined a support group. Posted in a cafe between a tarot reader's number and tear sheets for a '78 Toyota

('Runs good;' translation: suitable for use as artificial reef), the ad buzzed in my head like a june bug: 'how nice if we could realize our dreams.' If caffeine can sell lines like that, it makes you wonder why advertisers don't just scent *everything* with coffee. Even perfume spreads. Forget about impregnating magazines with cologne, just have French roast curling off Halle Berry's cleavage for Revlon. Creamer, anyone?

For better and worse, the support group propelled me into coffee's *klatches*. Weekly narratives about embezzlement and leg monitors, aired to strains of Windham Hill and herbal tea, left me ripe for addiction. At that point I met Marsha, a coffee connoisseur. Together we spiralled upward into caffiene dependency.

Fortunately, unlike Sid and Nancy or Ringo and Barbara, we ended neither sordidly nor in rehab. We didn't lose our house, jobs or cars—yet. The caffiene bug is a lot easier to shake than other habits.

Charge cards, for instance. We still haven't figured out how to put those in a drawer and forget about them.

In the Country
of No Butt

The advent of middle age has led me to ponder deep and resonant metaphysical questions, such as: what would life be like with a respectable tush?

Rear end-wise, I have often been one, and not infrequently had my head so far up my own that I could serve as my own proctologist, but I have never had one to speak of. No male in my family, dating back to Ethelred the Mungbat, has had one. It's not part of our gene pool. Great hair, teeth you could mine diamonds with, but no butt.

Unlike other epidermal features, behinds aren't necessarily subject to the gravitational pull that accompanies age and encourages these parts to migrate elsewhere. Breasts sag, bellies swell, hair gets thin on top and relocates to ears, upper lip, back, but arses stay put. If you're lacking in booty, there's no hope of it being augmented; it will remain unleavened buns. Frankly, if I were an ass—speaking literally this time—I'd be downright despondent at seeing the gut inches away expanding while I stayed flat.

The Fresh Prince of Back Hair: Intimations of Mortality

I don't exactly lose sleep over this, but it would be nice, say, not to endure uncomplimentary mammalian nomenclature from the women in your life—'saggy baggy elephant,' 'cow's udder,' and most degrading of all, 'monkey butt,' to which not one but two wives have subjected me. Or to shop for trousers without enduring lame exchanges with clerks over derriere deficiency. Nice, indeed, to find gear that actually hung right instead of looking like my diaper needed changing.

The only time my pants ever fit, in fact, was back in the late sixties, when the drainpipe look was popular. Pants then were like a second skin—you didn't so much wear them as mummify yourself in them. If you shifted in them the wrong way you risked hitting an impromptu high C. They were the closest thing to tights men ever wore and, with their tendency to bag at the knees, probably stimulated development of superior hosiery, not to mention outstanding control of bodily functions: once you were into them that was it, until you molted them at night.

Even without drainpipe trousers, being butt-challenged can be downright painful. I can't imagine what it would be like to sit at a ballgame (or in any unpadded seat) for longer than three minutes and not feel like a crocodile was devouring my keester. Aluminum bleachers—the ones with ridges, like high school football stadiums have—are the worst. Whoever designed those suckers must (A) have an ass that would safely cushion a destroyer dockside or (B) be the booster club president for a team with a losing streak that predates jockstraps and wants to make sure fans stay on their feet rooting.

I'm waiting for someone to invent an inflatable butt. It would work like a pneumatic brassiere. You'd carry a little pump with you and increase or diminish your booty to suit the circumstances. If you wanted, say, to gain the attentions of women in a

Obviously, we're talking about men. Women become conscious of the downside of aging sooner, when they leave the hospital after birth. *Theirs.* Female infants generally walk first because they're so anxious to get to the phone to order exfoliant and moisturizer from the *Shopping Channel* to keep their skin soft and wrinkle-free. Double-digit birthdays to them are just another headstone for dead cells.

Because guys hoof it more slowly toward oblivion awareness, when the DDBs do hit home they hit like a tornado, whirling you clean out of the Kansas of complacency. You start noticing what you're missing (or think you're missing), wondering if you can live (die) without it. If it's worth the effort to attain. If, in fact, it's now beyond reach. Depending on how opportunistically you've lived, this can be like getting tattooed with a bottlecap.

The categories of perceived deprivation that normally strike men my age are sex, toys (sex toys?), career, and image. The first three I've made peace with, at least until I start passing kidney stones like a Gatling gun.

I'm not planning to pursue the French-cutoffed teen down the block with legs that start where her coppery tresses end and the father who could bench press my armoire. I had enough of doing other people's homework in high school. I also can't afford tickets to see N' Synch.

I'm reconciled for now to not owning the only car I ever lusted after, a Chevelle Super Sport. I used to wash one every day in tenth grade: I'd drool on it, and the kid who owned it would wipe it off with my face. Until we acquire a driveway wider than two popsicle sticks and I upgrade my mechanical expertise, which currently runs to bungee cords and duct tape, I'm content to do donuts with coffee.

As for career change—middle-aged men can make the most bizarre leaps of faith. Schooled in rocket science, they suddenly leave NASA to play blues harp in a drag show. Not me. Not only do strapless gowns hit me in the chest wrong, walking the job plank to pursue one's bliss has certain drawbacks, such as (1) no income, (2) no food, (3) no Funniest Home Videos. The older you get, the less privation appeals. Sometimes I still think it'd be a gas to be a folksinger. Then I think about sleeping in the back of a beater with my arms around a twelve-string for months on end, beer for breakfast, shaving in a hubcap, and I flip the channel to VH-1 to catch Indigo Girls.

Which leaves image. This one's the killer. By the time you're fifty, the saying goes, you have the face you deserve. I'm almost there. So what did I do to deserve glacial grooves around my eyes? 'You must smile a lot.' Yeah, right. More likely they're from all the squinting I'm doing as my eyes go bad. Which isn't helping my brow, either. You've seen pictures of thatched cottages in England? My brow has drooped so much as I've aged, and my eyebrows grown so bushy, I could hire myself out as a portable Lake District to indigent Wordsworthians.

But if you really want to know what's bugging me about my self these days, what had me so depressed on my forty-fourth, it's . . . my voice. That's right. It's gotten progressively more nasal and hoarse. I used to sound like a sheep. Now I sound like a sheep gargling inside a trash can. I long for mellifluous golden tones, and all I get is a barnyard. Forget about a facelift; I want a voice lift.

Of course, doing that might mean I'd be tempted to acquire an SS 396 and hit the trail with a Fender and Goldilocks up the street.

Bahh humbug.

My speech therapist was more circumspect. She listened, recorded, gave me diagrams of facial muscles and techniques to relax them, lists of words and phrases to help enunciation. I learned I could be the *masseter* of my verbal fate.

'Pay attention to how you say 'goodbye,' she suggested. 'It's a good indicator of how you're forming sounds.'

'I never say goodbye,' I said. I was being truthful. Except for aping the rude flight attendants on *Saturday Night Live,* I hardly ever used the word. Farewells were never big in my house. My limey mother said 'cheerio.' Dad simply disappeared from view like a submarine. One minute he'd be standing over a heating grate slurping Grape-Nuts Flakes and milk, the warm air billowing his bathrobe, the next he'd be gone. We'd be alerted to his whereabouts only by snores from the bedroom.

It later occurred to me that a lot of people—parents, girl-friends, clients—had left, in one way or another, without saying goodbye, which meant that I hadn't, either. No wonder my jaw wouldn't open—it was crammed with all those unsaid partings.

That's changing, though. Bit by bit, the sheep is becoming, if not Henry Higgins, then Eliza Doolittle. Anna helps make sure of that. She no longer lets me walk her to the schoolbus in the morning—she's a big kid now—so every day I say goodbye to her from the curb. Goodbye to me as well. Loud and clear.

Run D.O.N.C.

One problem with getting older is that more things remind you that you're getting older. When you're young—say, on the windward side of thirty—the only thing that conveys a sense of mortality is how close to death you feel from a pitcher of margaritas. Fifteen years later, all kinds of things do that, jumping up and whacking you in the face like a garden rake you stepped on.

The death of family and friends always cracks your bridge. Suddenly, people you thought would accompany you every step of the way just aren't there anymore to block your view of the abyss. More insidiously, there's the death of idols—role models, or maybe just people you didn't know personally who goosed the status quo and made you feel, vicariously, more powerful.

To some extent, rock stars have been exempt from this kind of melancholy among their fans because of the nature of their profession—live fast, flame out early. You almost expect them to die young, so when they do, the myth tempers your grief. Oftentimes, your sense of loss is further diluted, if not eclipsed, by the manner of their passing, which can appear the final fruition of attitude. Let's face it, unless you burn incense to him at night, it's hard to be blown away with grief when a guitarist is found float-

174

ing face down in a jacuzzi full of gin, or impaled by an overdose. Though squalid, those almost qualify in the profession, in Native American lingo, as 'good' deaths. And when someone accidentally gets electrocuted onstage, you can almost hear cries of stoned approval from the audience.

Lately, though, a number of rock people have rent the veil of illusion surrounding them by dying of natural causes. That is, they violated the covenant with their fans by not only surviving into middle age, but succumbing to the same godawful illness that humped off Aunt Tillie. During the so-called glory days of rock, when someone like Jim Morrison got felled early by a heart attack, it was an understood byproduct of a debauched lifestyle. Shocking, but not necessarily lamented. Possibly even a good death.

But what's good about cancer, even if it does stem from youthful bad habits never rectified, such as cigarette smoking? Where's the romance in wasting away from substances that any Rotarian can indulge in?

In recent years the funeral cortege of popular musicians delineating the big C has stretched from here to Brixton: Mick Ronson, Nicky Hopkins, Sterling Morrison, Ben Orr, Laura Nyro, Joey and Johnny Ramone, George Harrison, Warren Zevon, Arthur Kane, Spencer Dryden, Jim Capaldi . . . sheesh. Does being wired to an amp automatically lower your t-cell count? Is it a question of electromagnetic radiation killing you, as with your cell phone? For good measure, the Great Promoter in the sky threw in a couple of heart failures, with John Entwistle and Joe Strummer. That list alone could comprise a posthumous rap group, Run D(ead) O(f) N(atural) C(auses). Not that they would chart anything, of course.

Ever get the feeling you've been cheated?

The Fresh Prince of Back Hair: Intimations of Mortality

Frankly, I never really expected aging rockers to be nineteen forever. But maybe a part of me pretended they were, so another part of me would feel ageless. And if I had to endure the occasional spectacle of them lumbering around the stage like a spavined Percheron, well, at least the spirit was still there, maybe more obvious than ever now shorn of the physical mystique of youth. *That* much wisdom I'll grant to age.

Sometimes I get the feeling the Great Promoter is sick of Boomer band reunions and is trying to prevent more of them. A Clash reunion without their frontman? No way. Maybe, ultimately, the common unplugging of our heroes will preserve the illusion of perpetual high decibel youth more than yet another Rolling Stones geriatric tour. For now, it's hard not to feel swindled when the noise is stilled so mundanely. No matter how good the show was, we want the encore to continue indefinitely.

Revenge of the
Sandwich Generation

The older I get, the more I think Rodney Dangerfield, even
though he belonged to a different generation, could serve as
a Baby Boomer poster boy. Because Boomers don't get no respect, or grudging respect at best.

Whoops, didn't mean to whine so much. For a minute
there, I sounded like Generation X.

Don't you love sociologists' tag names? The way they lump
millions of us together, as in an old Weegee photograph of Coney
Island? The Entitlement Generation, Boomers, Gen X. It's very
convenient, and done according to rigorous scientific principles
of demarcation, namely, sex. Boomers begin with millions of ser-
vicemen returning from WWII with a full payload, Xers about
when the diaphragm police stopped showing up, in the mid-'60's.
Entitlement people are the ones driving the van conversions that
ain't rockin' while stationary.

But to return. Intergenerational conflict is nothing new.
Throughout the ages each generation thinks the one that follows
it squanders the promise it inherited, and the younger one thinks
the older is clueless. The difference with Boomers is that we're
fair game for everybody.

Small wonder we're called the 'sandwich' generation. This image captures us beautifully, illustrating both our predicament and the contempt with which we're held; a true double-bind analogy. In the classic sense it refers to our being squeezed between taking care of our parents, who now are living long enough to acquire diseases that turn them into self-watering geraniums, and our own kids—which we're producing with less reckless abandon than they did—who are back living with us after their dot com enterprise went belly up. (You could also call us the 'herniated floppy disc' generation.)

It also connotes how we find ourselves skewered by these same parties. Ever notice the bumper stickers on those van conversions? WE'RE SPENDING OUR KIDS' INHERITANCE, a knock, presumably, at Boomers' materialism. Is it our fault our parents whetted our appetite with dreams of a leisure society? Get real. Don't feed us steak and then complain we don't want Alpo.

As for our kids, you'd think we'd favored a constitutional amendment for twentysomething circumcision rather than equal rights, environmental protection, and Aspartame. (Well, two out of three ain't bad.) With them living at home again, sharing our space and toys, it's just as well we're materialistic.

But the people who hate us most are politicians. They hate us because we're a problem that won't go away. Usually politicos love this kind of predicament because they can stall around indefinitely, milk it like a prize Holstein, table amendments and come back to it years later, giving the illusion of sustained effort without actually accomplishing anything. We're different: a problem with a deadline that carries very real consequences if it goes unsolved.

I'm referring, of course, to what will happen when the largest generation in American history begins to retire and no one has yet figured out how to prevent our bankrupting the Social Security system. Vis-à-vis social security, being a Boomer is like doing the wave at a ball game, except that 76 million of us are heading for shore at an alarming rate. Boomers are the demographic tsunami, with little ant-like politicians trying to surf down our face without getting swamped.

Actually, some of us are looking forward to the showdown. It's like being a kid and watching your dad saw a piece of wood on his workbench unawares that the vibration is causing a glass jar to creep ever closer to the edge. You stand there savoring the potential anarchy of the situation.

The day of our dotage will be a day of reckoning, a chance to get even for all the dissing. Our combined tendency toward constipation will be mirrored by the collective potential of the AARP to stall policies not in our favor. Manufacturers and advertisers who think they have our number will go mad trying to develop digital enema bags. Our children who mooched off us until they grew a new umbilical cord will have to put up with us appropriating their iPods. And if the Medicaid wards fill up we'll take to the road again, as we did in the sixties, dragging our IV drips and trading catheters for hearing aid batteries so we can hear Canned Heat again. There'll be no sitting around waiting for the pinch this time.

Better start buttering us up. No, make that light mayo, instead. Sandwichers have to watch the cholesterol.

Resolved

In length and anxiousness the line resembled photographs I'd seen of Ellis Island at the turn of the century.

The three of us were in a mall store in early December to have our picture taken. A happy family portrait to include in our Christmas cards.

The guy behind us had his dog with him. The dog had what looked like a dinner napkin around his neck and, possibly because they eat dogs in China, was eyeing Anna suspiciously.

Ahead of us a couple of twins were threatening to barf in unison if they didn't immediately remove their holiday finery. Their mother had nosed their stroller, about the size of a Hummer, into the fray, where it no doubt remains.

Anna herself, perhaps because her new tights kept falling down, was scarfing crackers as if to double her weight in time for the picture.

The only happy person on the premises was at the register. Occasionally a Brink's truck would arrive to take away the money she was collecting. While we waited she informed everyone that wallet sheets wouldn't be ready till the 21st. Obviously, she had never read *The Ox-Bow Incident*.

Resolved

Once in a geologic while a tectonic plate shifted and the line moved forward. As the sun set, our turn came. At the rear of the store a young woman positioned us in front of a snowflake backdrop. I reclined on my belly. Marsha sat next to me. And Anna, in a rare moment of acquiescence, plunked directly onto my sore lumbar.

At that moment I resolved to schedule next year's Christmas shoot around July 4th. So I could spend the holiday in a whirlpool.

While in line I thought of other things I could do to become sleek and prosperous in the months ahead.

(1) Move to Cameroon and become a cowherd. Just kidding.

(2) Play with Anna more, even if I need blood transfusions afterward. Her legs are like spring steel, and as with steel, you come off the worst in any encounter with them. She could teach kickboxing to pay for dance class.

(3) Watch more trash TV. How's this for a start? 'Totally Out of Control: Video segments show destructive and violent behavior of people in various situations. Hosted by Danny Bonaduce.' Must have been all those holistic moments with Shirley Jones.

(4) Follow more large people through crowds. They're like having an ice breaker around. Yesterday I was bucking a headwind downtown, leaning forward at a 45 degree angle, when I fell in behind two women who took up the entire sidewalk. And I mean *fell*, practically on my face, as they blocked the breeze. It made walking so easy I followed them ten blocks out of my way to an office furniture fire sale.

(5) Smile before noon, even if my jaw breaks. Smile at my neighbor cutting his grass while I'm trying to write. Smile at people who shove campaign literature at me. Smile at the auto teller

who truncates my name. Just so she doesn't rhyme it with bodily functions.

(6) Be kinder to my dentist. Not eat garlic before my exam, not squint at my x-rays as if they were torso murder pics, not ask if the Georgia O'Keefe print on his wall is titled *Epiglottis III*. So what if I could pay off my mortgage with what he makes during my visit? It's a rough job. Imagine looking up people's nostrils every day. Only proctologists have it worse. I mean, do dentists watch thousands of feet of nose hair footage to desensitize themselves, the way sex therapists watch porn movies?

(7) Quit more books. No more winching through turgid tomes about frontal lobe development in pygmies or subtext in Icelandic cinema. I need to learn how to program my cell phone.

See you at next year's holiday shoot. In my tank top.

Postscript

Not long ago I ran across a comment written by my late father on the flyleaf of one of his books. It read: 'Here's to the happiest days of my life, spent in the arms of another man's wife—my mother's.' The corn was typical—his humor was always knee-high by July. But what really hit me was the script itself, which I hadn't seen in years. Its stilted uniform strokes, like a series of clothespins, brought him and his angular ways rearing up before me again like Hamlet's ghost.

It made me wonder how *my* handwriting will be perceived after my demise in forty—make that fifty—years. Will someone open my old anthologies at a library sale, observe my cramped marginalia, and wonder if I kept my underpants wrapped in pink tissue paper? If I had names for my houseplants? (No to both, though I do have choice monikers for flora that dies on me.)

When we think of what survives us, we don't often consider penmanship. We focus on deeds and descendants, the paver purchased in the new stadium terrace, the shot of us with a trophy muskellunge. But the humble penstroke, with its habits and quirks, can 'fix' our image for posterity as well as any photograph. The circle-dotted 'i' or loopy dipthong is a trumpet blast of temperament that echoes through the years long after the hand that wrote it is written off.

For better or worse, not many things individualize you like handwriting. You may as well be writing in blood as ink. George Szell, a conductor so ruthless in his attention to detail that members of the Cleveland Orchestra preferred eating the score to hitting wrong notes, once discovered some mutinous graffiti about himself in a men's room stall backstage. He promptly hired a handwriting expert to finger the culprit, whose head was used as a wood block in the percussion section the rest of his career.

My own script suggests a Haldol habit. I write as if my hand is in a cast, all characters the same size and clinging to the line for dear life; basically, as I did in fifth grade. Hopefully this doesn't prefigure hearing messages from aliens later in life. For all its uniformity no one can read my writing, so I print. I'd rather be asked if I'm a draftsman than if I still live with my mother.

Ironically, illegible handwriting is often a hallmark of professionalism. As people climb the career ladder their script moves the other way, flattening out. Physicians' handwriting, for example, could pass for an EKG printout. It's as much a component of modern health care as the eight minute office visit, and the reason many pharmacists now minor in Egyptology. Despite pleas for doctors to write prescriptions as if they weren't expecting an air raid any second, years from now some of us probably will still be getting Perganol instead of Percodan, with a lot more kids than we bargained for.

Meantime, handwriting style across the blotter is going the way of the doubleheader. Scrawled legal pad notes, memos, lists and daily minder jottings now comprise most of our written messages. Leisurely letter writing, long a bastion of distinctive longhand, has been whittled to the riffing of chat rooms and e-mail. The visual appeal of script seems quaint as a spray of lavender in a saved opera libretto. As Post-Its and pixels replace the intimacy of penmanship, handwriting may no longer convey us as acutely to future generations. The portrait of us once left by old correspondence will become a connect-the-dots sketch joined by randomly surviving ephemera. The corn inside a musty copy of Tennyson's *Poems,* like the grain found in tombs of ancient Egyptians, will acquire archival significance, serving its author in an afterlife.

Who'da thunk it?

Order Form

Name: _____

Mailing Address: _____

City & State: _____

Zip Code: _____

Telephone: _____

Fax: _____

E-mail: _____

Please send _____ copy(s) of Breakfast at Noon: Backwards in the 'Burbs @ $14.95 per copy, plus $3.95 shipping ($1.95 for each additional copy)

Please bill my credit card.
Credit card: ❏ Visa   ❏ MC   ❏ Amex   ❏ Discover

Card No: _____

Exp date: _____

Signature of cardholder: _____

Code: _____

Please mail your order form to:
BookMasters, Inc.
30 Amberwood Parkway
Ashland, OH 44805
800-247-6553

You may fax your order to: 419-281-6883

E-mail your order to: order@bookmasters.com

Order through our web site: http://www.atlasbooks.com

About the Author

Proof that a mind divided against itself can still stand, C. R. Yeager has lived his entire life in and around Cleveland, Ohio. He has survived Mayor Perk's flaming hair, the blizzard of '78, various pro sport mistakes by the lake (Red Right 88, the Drive, Fumble, Shot, and Error), and zebra mussels. To his immense relief, he continues to be self-employed. When not corresponding with family in Stratford-Upon-Avon, England, he can be found devouring televised soccer games and ethnic food with wife Marsha and daughter Anna.